Frontispiece: *Self Portrait*. 1892. Oil on board, 14 x 11″. Collection Mr. and Mrs. Sidney F. Brody, Los Angeles

Edouard Vuillard

by Andrew Carnduff Ritchie

The Museum of Modern Art, New York

in collaboration with

The Cleveland Museum of Art

Printed in the United States of America
Library of Congress card number: 54-6136

Contents

Acknowledgments

On behalf of the Trustees of the Museum of Modern Art and the Cleveland Museum of Art, I wish to extend grateful acknowledgment to Claude Roger-Marx, André Chastel and Jacques Salomon, the three French writers who have done most in recent years to estimate and to reveal Vuillard's contribution to the art of our time. Without their researches and their accounts growing out of personal contacts with the artist, this study could not have been made. Each of them has generously assisted me in a number of ways.

I am grateful also to William S. Lieberman for his excellent notes on Vuillard as a printmaker; to Miss Alice Bacon, Miss Ellen Mary Jones and Miss Alicia Legg, of the Department of Painting and Sculpture, for assistance in research and in translations of quoted material; to Alfred H. Barr, Jr., Monroe Wheeler and Miss Margaret Miller for reading my manuscript and making a number of valuable suggestions; to Mme Jacqueline Bouchot-Saupique, Louis Carré, Ralph F. Colin, Philip James, M. Knoedler & Co., Jacques Lindon, Helmut Lütjen, Porter McCray, William M. Milliken, Mlle Marcel Minet, Frank Perls, John Rewald, J. Rodrigues-Henriques, Paul Rosenberg, Siegfried Rosengart, Sam Salz, Miss Darthea Speyer, Mme H. O. Van der Wal, Daniel Wildenstein, Miss Lelia Wittler and Charles Zadok for help in locating pictures and for many other courtesies; and to the many museum directors in this country and abroad who took time to answer a question regarding Vuillards in their vicinity.

Above all, I am indebted to Hanna Fund, Cleveland, Ohio, and to the lenders to the exhibition. Their generous cooperation has made possible the first extensive showing of Vuillard's paintings and prints in this country.

ANDREW CARNDUFF RITCHIE

Edouard Vuillard

Edouard Vuillard was a strangely complex personality. Many of the secrets of his life will be revealed in 1980 when, by his will, his private journal can be made public. Until then we must depend on the accounts of his friends and the evidence of his art for whatever estimates we may make of him. His origins were petty bourgeois and, despite his later associations with a somewhat fashionable set in Parisian society, he remained in all essentials a petty bourgeois to his death. He was a retiring, silent, even timid little man, given only occasionally to bursts of anger. He suffered from a kind of melancholy or ennui, which he endured patiently. He was a great reader on art and was devoted to the poetry of Mallarmé; he read Paul Valéry, Jean Giraudoux and all of Baudelaire.[1] Devoutly religious in his youth, he retained throughout his life something of the Jansenist Catholic's respect for the homely Christian virtues of simplicity, sobriety and honesty. Yet he was not a puritan. He enjoyed good living and, while he remained a bachelor all his life, it is rumored that he had several love affairs. But, as became his upbringing, he seems never to have allowed passion of any kind to get out of hand. Nothing, apparently, was permitted to disturb the even course of the ménage he kept with his mother until her death in 1928.

His quiet, introspective nature was respected and admired by all his friends. He was a listener rather than a talker and, perhaps because he preferred to paint rather than to theorize about painting, he retained the friendship of everyone in his circle. But however inarticulate he may have appeared at artist discussions, he clearly had a mind of his own. Maurice Denis, one of his boyhood friends, wrote in 1898 to Vuillard from Rome and said, among other things: "The value of a work of art lies in the plenitude of the artist's effort, in the force of his will." Vuillard's answer is a better characterization of himself than perhaps any critic or fellow painter has given us. He replied: "I suffer too much in my life and my work from what you speak of, not to reply immediately ... It is not while I am working that I think of the technique of picture making or of immediate satisfaction. To speak generally—it is not while I am doing this or that, that I consider the quality of my actions (you have only to think of my diffidence and my character). Whatever I have the happiness to be working at, it is because there is an idea in me in which I have faith. As to the quality of the result, I do not worry myself . . . I conceive, but in fact I actually experience only very rarely, that will and effort of which you like to speak. You have so

1 Thadée Natanson. *Peints à leur tour*, Albin Michel, Paris, 1948, p. 377.

long been accustomed by nature, education and circumstances and in presence of certain results that please you, to give a particular sense to the word *will* that you attempt to explain others, me for instance, by your own logic. You may sometimes deceive yourself. The important thing is that I have faith enough to produce. And I admit one could call that work. In general, I have a horror or rather a blue funk of general ideas which I haven't discovered for myself, but I don't deny their value. I prefer to be humble rather than pretend to understanding."[1]

Vuillard achieved an almost instantaneous success as a young painter in the '90s. After about 1905, however, for various reasons, his art began to attract less and less critical appreciation and by 1914 he withdrew almost completely from public exhibitions. It was not until 1936 that a considerable number of his early paintings was placed on exhibition and even so the occasion was an historical rather than a contemporary one—a review of the artists with whom he had been associated in his youth. In 1938, two years before his death, he was rather unwillingly induced to supervise the selection of a large retrospective exhibition of his work held at the Musée des Arts Décoratifs, and here many saw for the first time the full extent of his art and, particularly, the series of large decorative panels which had been hidden away in private houses. Since this exhibition, and especially since the last war, there has been a significant revival of interest in him. The 1938 exhibition undoubtedly inspired some of this interest. More important, perhaps, a revival of interest between the wars in the symbolist movement coincided with the revelation of Vuillard's distinctive contribution to it.

Vuillard was born in 1868 in Cuiseaux, Saône-et-Loire, the youngest child of a family of three. His father, a retired military officer, died in 1883, when Vuillard was fifteen. The family, meanwhile, had moved to Paris. His mother, a native of Paris, and twenty-seven years younger than her husband, decided on his death to occupy herself and support her family by going into business as a dressmaker. Her love and knowledge of the materials of her craft, which she was to transmit to her artist son, she must have come by directly. Her father and brother were both textile designers. Her workshop, where she employed two assistants, was first on the rue Daunou, and later in a room of the family apartment, on the ground floor of a house on the rue du Marché-Saint-Honoré.[2]

Vuillard's first school was one run by a Catholic teaching order, the Marist Brothers. He next attended the Ecole Rocroy and finally the Lycée Condorcet. It was the family intention to have him follow his father into the army by pre-

1 Quoted by Claude Roger-Marx. *Vuillard,* Editions de la Maison Française, New York, 1946, p. 20.

2 Vuillard and his mother remained at this apartment until 1896. They then moved to the rue Truffaut, in the Batignolles quarter, and afterwards to the rue de la Tour, near the Trocadero. Finally, after 1908, they moved to a house on the Square Vintimille. All of these addresses, it will be noted, are in a fairly restricted orbit and all are in quiet, middle-class districts.

paring him for the army college at St. Cyr. But his friends, and possibly the teaching at the Lycée Condorcet, decided him on an artist's course. Mallarmé taught English there until 1884, and it is of interest to note that Marcel Proust a few years later attended the same school. Vuillard's immediate school friends were Ker-Xavier Roussel, who was to marry his sister; Maurice Denis, whose interest in art profoundly influenced him; and Lugné-Poë, who was to become one of the most dynamic actor-managers of the Paris theatre of the '90s and who came to serve as an enthusiastic liaison between the writer and painter symbolists of his day.

Roussel, whom he met in 1884, was Vuillard's closest friend and it was he who seems to have influenced him most and got him to study at the Ecole des Beaux Arts, beginning in 1886, where Gérôme conducted one of the master classes. Growing discontented with the school and the teaching there, they joined forces in 1888 with a group of young rebel students at the Académie Julian, where Bouguereau was the chief teacher. This group, which included Maurice Denis, Sérusier, Bonnard, Ibels, Piot, Séguin, Vallotton and Ranson, banded together and early in 1889 called themselves the Nabis, a name derived from the Hebrew word for prophet. They were later joined by Maillol and the Dutch painter, Verkade. Their principal spokesmen were Sérusier and Denis.

Young Girl Seated. 1891. Brush drawing, 7⅛ x 7⅛". Collection John Rewald, New York

Vuillard seems at first to have been somewhat skeptical of all the enthusiastic theorizing indulged in by his friends. His first paintings of the years 1887-90 are more sensitive to atmosphere and texture than the academic realism of the schools. But they are still very conservative in drawing and restrained in color, by Nabi standards. His *Self Portrait with Varocquez* (p. 29) and the *Self Portrait in a Mirror* (color plate, p. 11), particularly the latter, suggest an early admiration for Degas, one that was to continue all his life and was, in fact, reciprocated by the older painter. The still lifes of these early years are usually studies of fruit, flowers and bottles (p. 30). They show a precise delicacy of perception and a sobriety of composition that remind one of Fantin-Latour, Chardin and possibly Vermeer. There are indications, too (color plate, p. 15), especially in the brushwork of some of these still lifes, that he had studied Manet and the impressionists and also Cézanne. The influence of the latter he may have acquired through his Nabi admiration for Cézanne's disciple, Gauguin. But he was at this time still a student, absorbing from a variety of sources whatever technical means he could. When asked once what had led him to become a painter, he replied: "I should like to say as Degas did: on Sundays they took us to the Louvre—my brother slid on the floors and I looked at the pictures."[1]

About 1890 Vuillard reached a crisis in his early career. In this year Bonnard occupied a small studio at 28 rue Pigalle, and Vuillard joined him there together with Maurice Denis and Lugné-Poë. He apparently could no longer deny the almost religious fervor of his friends. The symbolist movement, with which the Nabis were in sympathy, was then at its height. Mallarmé in poetry and Gauguin in painting were two of its leaders. In some ways a latter-day revival of the romantic movement of the first half of the nineteenth century, it sought to counter the documentary realism of the naturalist movement in letters, typified by the novels of Zola, and the literal translation of visual sensations by the impressionist painters. At the same time it fought the neo-classic verse techniques of the academic poets, the so-called Parnassians, and the mechanical "finish" of academic painters like Bouguereau and Gérôme. Led by Sérusier, who has been called St. Paul to Gauguin's Christ, the Nabis derived their first inspiration from the latter's school of Pont Aven. Emile Bernard, the admirer of Cézanne, was with Gauguin there and he, more than anyone in the Pont Aven circle, provided the theoretical basis for most of the master's anti-impressionist theories. In any case, Sérusier returned in 1888 from a summer in Brittany, bringing with him a cigar box lid on which he had demonstrated Gauguin's principles of flat, boldly outlined areas of color, signifying by their transformation and deformation of natural forms and colors the liberty of the individual artist to interpret nature according to his expressive needs. However much these principles of Gauguin may owe to the example of the Japanese print, which the impressionists had been responsible for bringing into fashion

1 Quoted by Claude Roger-Marx. *Opus cit.*, p. 15.

Self Portrait in a Mirror. 1888-90. Oil on canvas, 17½ x 21⅛″. Collection Sam Salz, New York

at this time and which for Gauguin, with his penchant for the primitive and the exotic, must have had a double appeal, the fact remains that Gauguin by his messianic fervor was primarily responsible, through Sérusier, for the inception of the Nabi-symbolist theories. Furthermore, the large representation of his work in the *Peintres synthétistes et symbolistes* exhibition in 1889 at the Café Volpini provided the young Nabis with a wealth of demonstration of these same theories.

Vuillard's reaction to these symbolist theories, which were also called synthetist and neo-traditionist, is to be seen in his paintings of 1890-92; for example, *The Dressmakers* (p. 32), *Little Girls Walking* (color plate, p. 17), and *The Wood* (p. 31). They demonstrate his brilliant application of Gauguin's advice to Sérusier: "How does that tree look to you? Green? All right, then use green, the greenest green on your palette. And that shadow, a little bluish? Don't be afraid. Paint it as blue as you can!"[1] In the narrow range of his palette in these early pictures Vuillard also is following Gauguin's advice. According to Verkade, Gauguin "taught with Goethe that the artist first of all shows his strength in the limitation of his materials. Hence he allowed his pupils at first the use of only five or six colors—Prussian blue, madder-lake, cinnabar, chrome-yellow or cadmium, yellow ochre and white."[2] And surely Vuillard followed during these same years Maurice Denis' now famous dictum announced in 1890: "Remember that a picture—before being a battle horse, a female nude or some anecdote—is essentially a flat surface covered with colors assembled in a certain order."[3] In fact, Vuillard went Denis one better and avoided battle horses and anecdotes altogether and only rarely, and later in his career, painted a nude. In short, he took from the synthetist credo only its technical formulations on color and drawing and, unlike all the other Nabis with the exception of his friend Bonnard, avoided the anecdotal, peasant subjects inspired by Gauguin or the Pre-Raphaelite-like primitivism of Maurice Denis' religious pictures.

Like Bonnard he chose to stick to the world he knew intimately, in his case his home and his mother's workroom or, if he went outdoors, the familiar parade of people in the parks and gardens of Paris. This choice of subject matter has, in fact, a closer relation to the impressionists than to the symbolists. Vuillard may have known at this time an article by the impressionist critic Duranty, published in 1876 and republished in 1946 with a prefatory note saying that Vuillard had brought it to the publisher's attention. Duranty writes:

"There is for every observer a logic of color and of drawing which proceeds from an aspect, according to whether it is caught at some hour, some season, some place. This aspect is not expressed, this logic is not determined by placing Venetian materials

1 Maurice Denis. *Paul Sérusier. ABC de la Peinture, Sa Vie—Son Oeuvre*, Paris, Librairie Floury, 1942, p. 42.

2 Dom Willibrord Verkade. *Yesterdays of an Artist Monk*, New York, 1930, p. 68.

3 Maurice Denis. *Théories, 1890-1910*, Paris, 1912, p. 1. (Article first published in *Art et Critique*, 1890.)

against Flemish backgrounds, by making studio lights shine on old chests and vases. [Duranty here criticizes the practice of the academic painters of his day.] It is necessary to avoid, if one wishes to be truthful, mixing times and environments, hours and light sources. The velvety shadows, the golden lights of Dutch interiors come from the structure of the houses, from the small-paned, mullioned windows, from streets on steamy canals. With us the values of tones in interiors play with infinite variety, according to whether one is on the first or the fourth floor, whether the house is heavily furnished and carpeted, or whether it is sparsely furnished; thus, an atmosphere like a family air is created in each interior between the furniture and the objects that fill it. The frequency, the multiplicity and the disposition of the mirrors which ornament the apartments, the number of objects which run up against the walls—all these things have brought into our homes either a kind of mystery or a kind of light which can no longer be represented by Flemish means or harmonies, like adding Venetian formulae, nor by the combinations and arrangements that can be imagined in the best planned studio . . .

"The language of the empty apartment must be sufficiently clear so that one may deduce the character and the habits of those who live in it; and the street will tell by its passers-by what time of day it is, what moment of the public life is represented.

"The appearances of things and of people have a thousand ways of being unforeseen in reality. Our point of view is not always in the center of a room with its two lateral walls running toward that of the background; the lines and angles of cornices do not always meet with regularity and mathematical symmetry; one is not always free to suppress the expanding space in the foreground; it is sometimes very high, sometimes very low, losing the ceiling, picking up objects below, cutting off furniture unexpectedly. Our eye stops at the side at a certain distance from us, seems restricted by a frame, and it does not see the lateral objects that are caught in the margin of the frame.

"From within, it is through the window that we communicate with the outside; the window is still a frame which accompanies us without cease, lasting while we are in the house, and this time is considerable. The frame of the window, according to whether we are far from it or near it, whether we are seated or standing, cuts off the outside scene in the most unexpected, the most changing manner, procuring for us the eternal variety, the spontaneity which is one of the great zests of reality."[1]

Vuillard may well have been influenced by this impressionist approach to reality, but he added another dimension to his perception of it. Bonnard was closer to Duranty's conceptions. He depicts the Parisian scene with a child-like joy in the ever-changing patterns of movement along the streets and boulevards —discovering a new picturesqueness in ordinary, everyday sights. Vuillard's eye and temperament found a different meaning in the common things about him. Having explored to his complete satisfaction the extreme possibilities of the redness of red, the greenness of green, the blueness of blue, and having "assembled" his colors in a striking variety of orders, retaining to the full the flatness of his panel or canvas, he proceeded to explore as early as 1893, in what one feels is a Mallarméan spirit, the mysterious possibilities of an infinite gradation of color hues to extract thereby the subtlest overtones, the essential perfume of intimate objects and activities in and about his home. The progressive toning down of his earlier juxtapositions of bright areas of color to an almost

1 Edmond Duranty. *La Nouvelle Peinture. A propos du Groupe d'Artistes qui expose dans les Galeries Durand-Ruel.* (1876) New Edition, with foreword and notes by Marcel Guérin, Librairie Floury, Paris, 1946, pp. 44-46.

Mallarmé. c. 1896. Drawing. Private collection, Paris

whispered chorus of low notes in a minor key reminds one of the lines from a poem of Verlaine's, quoted by Huysmans in *A Rebours:*

> *Car nous voulons la nuance encore*
> *Pas la couleur, rien que la nuance*
> . . . .
> *Et tous le reste est littérature.*[1]

Mallarmé, speaking of the Parnassians, the academic poets of his time, said that they "take the thing just as it is and put it before us—and consequently they are deficient in mystery: they deprive the mind of the delicious joy of believing that it is creating. To name an object is to do away with the three quarters of the enjoyment of the poem which is derived from the satisfaction of guessing little by little: to suggest it, to evoke it—that is what charms the imagination."[2]

Vuillard was very familiar with these ideas of Mallarmé. He attended the famous Tuesday evenings in the poet's apartment on the rue de Rome.[3] He was sufficiently intimate with him to have painted his house at Valvins at least four

1 "For what we still desire is the nuance/Not the color, nothing but the nuance/And all the rest is literature."

2 Quoted by Edmund Wilson. *Axel's Castle*, Charles Scribner's Sons, New York, 1931, p. 20.

3 To these Tuesday evenings there also came, at one time or another, Whistler, Degas, Huysmans, Paul Valéry, André Gide, Oscar Wilde, Remy de Gourmont, Arthur Symons, George Moore and W. B. Yeats. How many of these artists and writers Vuillard met is not certain. We do know he admired Degas and knew André Gide.

Bottle with Flowers. (La Bouteille avec des fleurs.) 1889-90. Oil on canvas, 12½ x 15¾″. Collection Mr. and Mrs. Donald S. Stralem, New York

times (p. 53); and that their respect for each other was considerable is indicated by the fact that Mallarmé seriously considered having Vuillard illustrate his major dramatic poem, *Hérodiade.*

The secret charm of so many of Vuillard's small panels of the '90s is the result of his never quite "naming" an object, as Mallarmé puts it. He "suggests" it, he "evokes" it, by knitting it into an amazingly complex tapestry. And by a process of telescoping planes in a picture, for example the *Interior at l'Etang la Ville,* Roussel's home (p. 48), or *Mother and Baby* (color plate, p. 49), the foreground, middleground and background overlap and fuse into a pulsating space that bears a kind of relation to the fusion of imagery in a poem by Mallarmé.

As with all the symbolists, Vuillard and Mallarmé insist upon the primacy of art over nature. And significantly, in order to emphasize and clarify the process of symbolic transformation of nature, Mallarmé (and here he is followed by Vuillard) chooses the simplest, most intimate objects in his room, a curtain, a vase or a lamp, and by an infinitely subtle fusion of allusive conceits "charms the imagination" into an almost occult state of detachment from the object, an object that had served only as a barely referred to point of departure.

Une dentelle s'abolit *Dans le doute du Jeu suprême* *A n'entr'ouvrir comme un blasphème* *Qu'absence éternelle de lit.*	A lace curtain stands effaced In doubt of the supreme game Unfolding like a blasphemy On eternal bedlessness.
Cette unanime blanc conflit *D'une guirlande avec la même,* *Enfue contre la vitre blême* *Flotte plus qu'il n'ensevelit.*	This unanimous white conflict Of a garland with its like Vanishing on the pallid glass Is floating more than burying.
Mais chez qui du rêve se dore *Tristement dort une mandore* *Au creux néant musicien*	But with him where dreams are gilt Sadly sleeps a mandola Whose hollow void is musical
Telle que vers quelque fenêtre *Selon nul ventre que le sien,* *Filial on aurait pu naître.*	Such that towards some window pane According to no womb but its, Filial one might be born.[1]

Vuillard's fusion of images is by no means as complex or, one might say, as strained as Mallarmé's. Nor is there in his little panels the depths of melancholy of the older poet. But there is in such pictures as the *Green Lamp* (p. 57), *The Room under the Eaves* (color plate, p. 45) and *Mystery* (p. 57) a haunting note of sadness, a mysterious gloom that is truly Mallarméan. And the very compactness of these pictures, their smallness, packed to the edges as they are with suggestive imagery, recall Mallarmé's compressed, highly concentrated short

1 Mallarmé. *Poems,* translated by Roger Fry, New Directions, New York, 1951, pp. 118-119.

Little Girls Walking. 1891. Oil on canvas, 32 x 25⅝". Collection Mr. and Mrs. Walter Ross, New York

poems. Above all, there is a Mallarméan narcissism in Vuillard's constant preoccupation not only with himself in his self portraits but, by extension, with his mother—reading, preparing meals, at work as a dressmaker, engaging in all the endless little activities of a bourgeois housewife. It is as if he sees in her and in the beloved furnishings and patterned walls of his home a constant reminder, a projection of his whole being. This is the mystery, this is the secret of Vuillard, as narcissism in varying degrees is the secret of all his fellow symbolists.

If, however, Mallarmé is the dominant poetic influence on Vuillard, the pervasive influence of Redon, whom Mallarmé admired and who, after Gauguin's departure for Tahiti, became the hero of the Nabis, must not be forgotten. Not that the strange, hallucinatory content of Redon's lithographs and etchings can be remotely connected with Vuillard's interiors on the rue du Marché-Saint-Honoré. Rather, as with Mallarmé, the symbolic implications of Redon's imagery and, technically, his mastery of infinitely subtle values in his prints and later in his pastels, appealed to the idealistic Nabis as a whole and to Vuillard in particular. Furthermore, Vuillard besides being a painter was, like Bonnard and Lautrec, a printmaker of great skill and tonal delicacy. And Redon was the acknowledged master of his craft, at least to Vuillard and his friends. Their respect for him as an artist was signalized by the predominantly Nabi exhibition organized by the critic André Mellerio at Durand-Ruel's gallery

Figure in a Room. c. 1891. Watercolor, 9½ x 5½″. Collection Mr. and Mrs. H. Lawrence Herring, New York

in 1899, when Redon was given the place of honor on the walls. And when Maurice Denis came to paint his *Hommage à Cézanne* in 1900, Redon was once again included among the Nabi brethren.

By contrast, the hothouse decadence of Gustave Moreau, the teacher of Rouault and Matisse, however much his paintings may have appealed to literary symbolists like Huysmans, seems to have been antipathetic to the Nabis as a group. There are many facets to the symbolist movement, but the Nabis did not find all of them congenial to their tastes. The Baudelaire-Edgar Allen Poe strain of decadence which had its effect upon Huysmans, Verlaine and Mallarmé was too perverse and too obsessed with evil to appeal to devout young Nabis like Denis and Vuillard. And Sérusier, however far his studies led him into Semitic literature (hence, probably, the Hebrew name Nabi for his friends), theosophy and the occult, never showed any inclination in his paintings to follow anyone other than Gauguin. The overtones of Baudelairean satanism in Mallarmé were perhaps too refined to have more than an unconscious influence upon his young admirers. In Vuillard's case it is hard to find more than melancholy echoes of this particular symbolist tradition. No matter how much the imagery of Mallarmé may have appealed to him or influenced him, or how much of Baudelaire he had read, there is no conscious expression of evil in his intimate little interiors.

It is at first sight a paradox that Vuillard, who so consistently painted small, tightly organized panels, often pieces of millboard no bigger than the cigar box lid brought back by Sérusier from Pont Aven, should at the same time have painted so many large decorative panels for the homes of his friends and patrons, among them Alexandre Natanson, one of the editors of the *Revue Blanche*, the novelist Claude Anet, and Dr. Vaquez. The paradox resolves itself, however, when we recall that one of the principal tenets of the Nabi credo, derived from Gauguin, was that all art is decoration. Albert Aurier, the young critic who was the Nabis' chief spokesman, at the conclusion of an article on Gauguin, insisted that a work of art should be: "... *decorative:* for decorative painting, properly speaking, as the Egyptians and probably the Greeks and the Primitives conceived it, is nothing but a manifestation of art at once subjective, synthetist, symbolist and ideist ... Painting can only have been created to decorate with thoughts, dreams and ideas the blank walls of human buildings. The easel picture is nothing but an illogical refinement invented to satisfy the fancy or the commercial spirit of decadent civilizations." And he concluded by complaining that the world had confined Gauguin to easel pictures, and had given him no walls, not even a hovel, to paint.[1]

Verkade, the Dutch painter who became a Nabi, tells us: "In the early part of 1890 the war cry went up from studio to studio: 'No more easel pictures! Away with useless bits of furniture! Painting must not usurp a freedom which cuts it off from the other arts! The painter's work begins where the architect

1 G. Albert Aurier. "Le Symbolisme en peinture," *Mercure de France*, March, 1891.

decides that his work is finished! Give us walls and more walls to decorate! Down with perspective! The wall must be kept as a surface, and must not be pierced by the representation of distant horizons. There are no such things as pictures, there is only decoration.' "[1]

Gauguin, whose ideas and example had fired an Aurier and a Verkade to these cries for wall decorations, had in his room at Pouldu in Brittany photographs of Manet's *Olympia*, Botticelli's *Birth of Venus*, an *Annunciation* by Fra Angelico, prints of the Japanese, Utamaro, and paintings of Puvis de Chavannes. It was from such diverse sources that the Nabis and, above all, Vuillard drew their inspiration for large decorative panels. And in Vuillard's case it is not hard to see, in the first series of panels done for Alexandre Natanson in 1894, how much he owes to Puvis and to Botticelli for his decorative scheme. One has but to compare Puvis' *Sacred Grove* in the Hemicycle of the Sorbonne and Botticelli's *Spring* with *Under the Trees* (color plate, p. 34). Vuillard has drawn from both his tree-defined intervals of space, the arabesque of figure and branch set off against the verticals of tree trunks, and the blocking out of the horizon by cutting the composition off at top and sides across the thickset mass of foliage. Each of these spatial devices Vuillard uses to achieve an all-over flatness of effect in order not to destroy or penetrate the wall he is decorating. And for the same reason, whether he paints in oil on canvas or distemper on millboard, his object, like Puvis' and like the Japanese print, or the flower decorated wallpaper that was the fashion in the '90s, is to achieve a juxtaposition of flat areas of mat colors which will deploy themselves evenly over a two-dimensional wall surface.

In some of Vuillard's panels, particularly his garden scenes, one other important influence is very marked—the early paintings of Claude Monet. *The Woman in the Garden* of 1867, now in the Louvre, is the direct ancestor of *The Park* (color plate, p. 37) and the *Woman Seated in a Garden* (p. 67). Monet's pattern of striped and spotted costumes, the elegant arabesques described by figures, skirts and foliage, the dappling of sunlight and shadow as a decorative device, the framing of the picture by the cutting of the trees at top and sides—all find a flattened, airless echo in Vuillard's paintings.

The sources of Vuillard's decorative style may be many, but the finished picture is his own. Actually, by his particular selection of decorative devices—his closed, hermetic compositions, his use of arabesque motifs, the all-over pattern of his designs—he made a notable contribution to a style that sprang into fashion in the '90s, *art nouveau*. We have too long thought of *art nouveau* as a style of ornament applied to furniture, objets d'art, architecture and book illustration. Insufficient attention has been given to the Nabis' emphasis upon wall decoration and the coalescence and interdependence of their ideas with those deriving from William Morris and the English Pre-Raphaelites and the Belgian *art*

1 Quoted by Daniel-Henry Kahnweiler, *Juan Gris, His Life and Work*, translated by Douglas Cooper, Curt Valentin, New York, 1947, pp. 67-68.

Lilacs. 1892. Oil on board, 14 x 11 1/8″. Collection Mr. and Mrs. Donald S. Stralem, New York

nouveau exponents, Van de Velde and Horta.[1] When the totality of Vuillard's decorative work of the '90s is properly appreciated, he may well be considered, in addition to his symbolist contribution, one of the outstanding *art nouveau* painters of his time.

In one thing Vuillard does not deviate in his decorative panels from his small paintings—the intimacy of his subject matter. His park scenes have a curious quality of the indoors about them, so enclosed and sheltered are the spaces he describes, so lacking in movement or drama are the incidents he observes—figures among the trees, almost as static as the trees themselves, a nursemaid with her charges, a woman reading in a garden, or simply sitting in a garden, figures in a room, and around a piano. Here he presents the quiet, ordinary relationships of the animate and the inanimate, the fusion of person and thing until both become one, and every shape, every color, every accent merges into a sustained tapestry-like rhythm comparable to the continuum of sound in a passage of Wagner or Debussy.[2]

André Gide, in his review of the 1905 *Salon d'Automne,* where Vuillard's masterpieces of decoration, the Vaquez panels (pp. 64, 65), were first publicly shown, said: "I do not know what I like most here. Perhaps, M. Vuillard himself. I know few works where one is brought more directly into communion with the painter. This is due, I suspect, to his emotion never losing its hold on the brush and to the outside world always remaining for him a pretext and handy means of expression. It is due to his speaking in a low tone, suitable to confidences, and to one's leaning over to listen to him . . . His melancholy is not romantic nor haughty, it is discreet and clothed in an everyday garment; it is caressingly tender, I might even say, timid, if this word were in consonance with such mastership. Yes, I see in him, his success notwithstanding, the charm of anxiety and doubt. He never puts forward a colour without excusing it by some subtle and precious withdrawal. Too modest to assert, he insinuates . . . No seeking for the showy, a constant search for harmony. By a grasp of relations, at once intuitive and studied, he explains each colour by its neighbor and obtains from both a reciprocal response . . . "[3]

When the cry first went up from the Nabi studios for walls to paint, one of the first responses seems to have come from Lugné-Poë, the actor-manager of the *Théâtre Libre* and the *Théâtre de l'Oeuvre* and an intimate friend of Vuillard, Bonnard and Maurice Denis. Lugné offered the young artists walls—the artificial walls of the stage—and all three designed and painted sets, for him and for Paul Fort's *Théâtre de l'Art,* with great enthusiasm. Unfortunately, these sets have long since been destroyed, and we can only imagine what, for example, Vuillard

1 In this connection it should be remembered that Tiffany showed stained glass windows at the *Salon* of 1895 after designs by Vuillard and other members of the Nabi group.

2 Both composers were admired by the Nabis. Wagner was indeed idolized by all the symbolists.

3 André Gide. "Promenade au Salon d'Automne," *Gazette des Beaux-Arts,* Dec. 1905, quoted from Claude Roger-Marx. *Opus cit.,* pp. 125-26.

designed for Ibsen's *Rosmersholm,* presented at the *Théâtre de l'Oeuvre* in 1893. Bonnard and another Nabi artist, Ranson, helped in the work. All we know is that Lugné-Poë said: "It was the scenery of the second act which stamped the note of intimacy and distinction on our set. Vuillard surpassed himself in ingenuity and economic invention in creating atmosphere and scenic decoration."[1] Vuillard with other Nabi artists also made lithographic designs for theatre programs, for example, one for Ibsen's *An Enemy of the People,* presented in 1893, and another for Maurice Beaubourg's *La Vie Muette,* in 1894 (p. 93). The most important theatre decorations by Vuillard, which are still happily in existence, were done not as stage sets but as decorations for the foyer of the *Comédie des Champs-Elysées.* While these were painted in 1913, long after Vuillard's first association with the theatre, they are the only major evidence we have of his devotion to the stage. The two largest panels illustrate scenes from Molière's *Le Malade Imaginaire* and Tristan Bernard's light comedy, *Le Petit Café* (p. 87). Brilliant as these panels are in the rendering of the atmosphere and lighting of the stage, the one extraordinary thing lacking in them is a sense of movement. It is as if Vuillard in both plays had been hypnotized by the scene rather than by the action and, following his own predilection for decoration, he froze the gestures of his actors in mid-air. The result is a curiously static performance—tableaux, without movement or words.

We have said that Vuillard's success was immediate in the '90s. A year older than Matisse and three years older than Rouault, he reached artistic maturity at least ten years before either of them. Like his admirer Toulouse-Lautrec, who was only four years his senior, his art reached an extraordinary degree of sophistication before he was thirty. He and his friend Bonnard, unlike so many of their fellow Nabis, "arrived" a bare four or five years after leaving art school. Both painters, like Lautrec again, are striking examples of the precociousness that was a characteristic of their *fin-de-siècle* period. And, surely because both preferred to paint rather than to theorize, they were able to apply the theories of their Nabi friends while the latter were still expounding them and worshipping at the shrine of Gauguin.

After 1900 the Nabis practically disbanded as a group. It is perhaps not fortuitous that their breakup almost coincided with the deaths of two of their heroes in 1898—Mallarmé and Puvis de Chavannes. The one represented their chief contact with the advanced literary figures of the day. Puvis, in his position as president of the Salon of the Société des Beaux-Arts, must have provided, by association, a certain cachet to the work and theories of the Nabi avant-garde. However that may be, after the dissolution, each of the Nabi brethren went his own way and, almost without exception, it was a way that ran counter to all the major movements of twentieth-century art. Sérusier, a too-devoted

1 Quoted by Claude Roger-Marx. *Opus cit.*, p. 18.

follower and imitator of Gauguin, was never quite able to divorce himself from the master's influence. As the years passed, his theories of painting became more abstruse and he became hopelessly involved in a numerological system of picture construction. Denis continued to write better than he painted and, no matter how increasingly devout he became, his decorative and religious paintings are but a weak expression of the intensity of his beliefs. And so with all the other Nabis except Bonnard. Verkade became a monk, and Roussel lost himself in a remote, repetitious version of Mallarmé's world of *L'Après-Midi d'un Faune*. Vallotton, whose early paintings of the '90s show something of the verve and subtlety of observation of Vuillard and Bonnard, became a stiff, tortured realist, reflecting in labored tightness of line and hard, metallic paint surface his puritan Swiss origins.

Inevitably, then, from the late careers of so many of the Nabis one gets a general feeling of frustration. Their idealistic, decorative program was so completely at odds with the temper and changing ideologies of the new century that all but one of them, Bonnard, found himself more or less stranded on the sidelines. Even Vuillard, perhaps the most brilliant of the Nabis, could not quite escape the fate of his friends.

One becomes conscious of a change in his work at the turn of the century. It is very gradual at first and is closely associated with a change about the same time in his social life. From the poetic tensions that so mark the Mallarméan years, 1893 to about 1900, he moves into a more relaxed, ostensibly less melancholy mood. His pictures reflect his new connections with a fashionable world as opposed to the old life of café discussions, literary inspiration and the close, germinal atmosphere of his own private existence at home. He now had an official dealer connection, the Bernheim brothers, and through an associate of theirs he was introduced to what must have appeared to him at first as a rather superficial company of friends, many of them, presumably, and intentionally, prospective clients. He was encouraged to paint "intimate" portraits of them, seated as casually as may be in their elaborately furnished rooms. These new interiors, larger, more elegant than those of his own home, seem to have demanded at once an increase in the scale of his panels or canvases. The old world of his own rooms and those of his sister, Mme Roussel, because they were so intimately known, so long-studied, could be compressed into a compass no bigger than ten by twelve inches. And by their very compression the intensity of their mysterious quality of intimacy was tremendously heightened. On the contrary, when he came to paint the interior of a client's house, one of his newfound fashionable friends, he found himself bound to relax his gifts of concentration, and in relaxing he enlarged his pictures accordingly.

The reduced tension is often charming. His looser brushwork and more obvious color arrangements often result in a delightful, even gay, picture which is far removed from the exquisite, brooding harmonies of many of his earlier, small panels. His decorative panels also are more loosely organized, more frankly decorative in the ordinary sense of the word. The impressionist, one

Mother and Sister of the Artist. c. 1893. Oil on canvas, 18¼ x 22¼″. The Museum of Modern Art, New York. Gift of Mrs. Sadie A. May

feels, has triumphed over the symbolist. Intimacy—the close observation and transformation of a restricted, hermetic view of things—has given place to a picturesque display of technical virtuosity.

The expansion of Vuillard's social contacts, which is so closely related to his larger pictures, his more fashionable interiors, is responsible too for his now leaving Paris during the summers and spending them with his new friends in Normandy and Brittany. The result is a vacation-like enjoyment of landscape and an attempt to record his impressions of the country and the sea. Probably again because he could never quite adjust his intimate genius to unknown territory, these views of fields and harbor scenes are often conventional and unexciting. The landscape beyond his favorite Square Vintimille and the parks of Paris are too foreign, it seems, too remote from his urban-provincial world to yield to his genius for compression and distillation. From the windows of his studio it is another story (p. 84). Here the roofs and streets of his district are as familiar, as well loved, as his favorite chair.

And when he returns from the salons of his friends to his mother seated at a window (color plate, p. 90), his ability to transform and transcend the ordinary by the alchemy of his affectionate spirit is immediately evident. Perhaps his affection for older women, like that for his mother, is responsible for the relative success of such a portrait as that of Mme Bénard (p. 89), whatever its pictorial failings may be in the somewhat insensitive overconcentration on meticulously rendered detail. So too when he turns from the overstuffed luxuriousness of upper middle-class rooms to subject matter completely removed from any "society" connotations, a doctor operating (p. 88), a dentist in his office (p. 89), or his artist friends at work or in their studios (p. 91), he is able for a moment to apply his eye and hand without reservations or artistic compromise. He comes to such scenes with a Degas-like perception of the unconventional pose or incident. However unintimate some of these scenes may be, in terms of his usual milieu, the fact that they were not commissions to record the ostentatious furnishings and persons of social clients must have acted as a spur to his imagination.

Nevertheless, when all is said by way of extenuation, and however one may try to select later work that reflects something of Vuillard's original genius, the fact remains that the progress of his art during the last twenty-five years of his life, until his death in 1940, appears to us now as retrogressive, if not reactionary. Despite his extraordinary craftsmanship as a painter, as he grew older and withdrew more and more into himself, he seems to have taken an almost perverse pleasure in denying his symbolist instincts—his wonderful ability to transform and synthesize the phenomena of natural appearances—and, in an excruciating effort to record the most minute detail, he came to sacrifice, more often than not, unity in his compositions and harmony in his color orchestrations.

His defeat, such as it was, is traceable to his vulnerability to an insensitive, materialist element in Parisian society that may be said to have exploited his talents. Undoubtedly, this society, whose values were vulgarized, corrupted an artist like Vuillard who chose to serve it. The choice, however, was Vuillard's and he cannot escape the final responsibility. It is true, as a few late pictures bear witness, that he struggled to retain something of his original intimacy of feeling. But, one feels, these occasional examples of an earlier privacy of expression are in the nature of nostalgic memories of a world long past. The economic and social upheavals of the present century must have frightened him as much as they did his fashionable friends. And, for much the same reasons that they were afraid of change, he must have looked with discomfort, not to say fear, at the tensions set up by the avant-garde art movements of our time. The fauve painters, for example, who were the sensation of the 1905 *Salon d'Automne,* however decorative their intentions, were too lusty, too enthusiastic admirers of van Gogh, to suit his symbolist inheritance. The cubist revolt derived from an appreciation of Cézanne's formal discoveries that seems to have been beyond the comprehension of Vuillard and the Nabis, however much they admired the older master as an anti-impressionist pioneer. And the surrealists, with their conscious exploration of the unconscious, must have offended Vuillard's sense of privacy, if nothing else.

One concludes that the quietist, intimate genius of Vuillard was too foreign to the spirit of these times, whether social or artistic, to have waged anything but a losing battle with forces that were apparently beyond his control. Nevertheless, the extraordinary quality and maturity of his early work can never be denied and it may well have a peculiar relevance for us today. Is there possibly some connection between the striving of a Vuillard to retain something of that inwardness, that self-searching narcissism which was the symbolist's answer in the '80s and '90s to the materialism of the impressionists and the academies, and the struggle of artists today to maintain their artistic integrity at all costs? "We have lived," as Churchill has said, "through half a century of the most terrible events which have ever ravaged the human race."[1] As disillusionment has followed these tragic events, the individual has been forced in on himself in an attempt to discover some personal standards on which to base his conduct. The sensitive artist has likewise felt compelled to formulate, or express himself through, an increasingly personal imagery. Vuillard's private world of images, derived from the objects and persons intimately associated with him, may take on a new meaning, then, in the light of present-day artists' needs and desires. And in the same way that symbolist poets like Verlaine and Mallarmé have had a profound influence on twentieth-century poets, it is possible that the symbolist values of Vuillard's "intimate" paintings still have a potential significance for painters today.

1 Speech at Margate, England, October 10, 1953.

Symphony in Red. 1893. Oil on board, 23 x 25¾″. Collection Mr. and Mrs. Ralph F. Colin, New York

Vuillard and his Friend Varoquez. 1888-90. Oil on canvas, 36 x 28″. Collection Alex Lewyt, New York

Still Life. 1889-90. Oil on canvas, 18 x 25½″. Collection Mr. and Mrs. Nate B. Spingold, New York

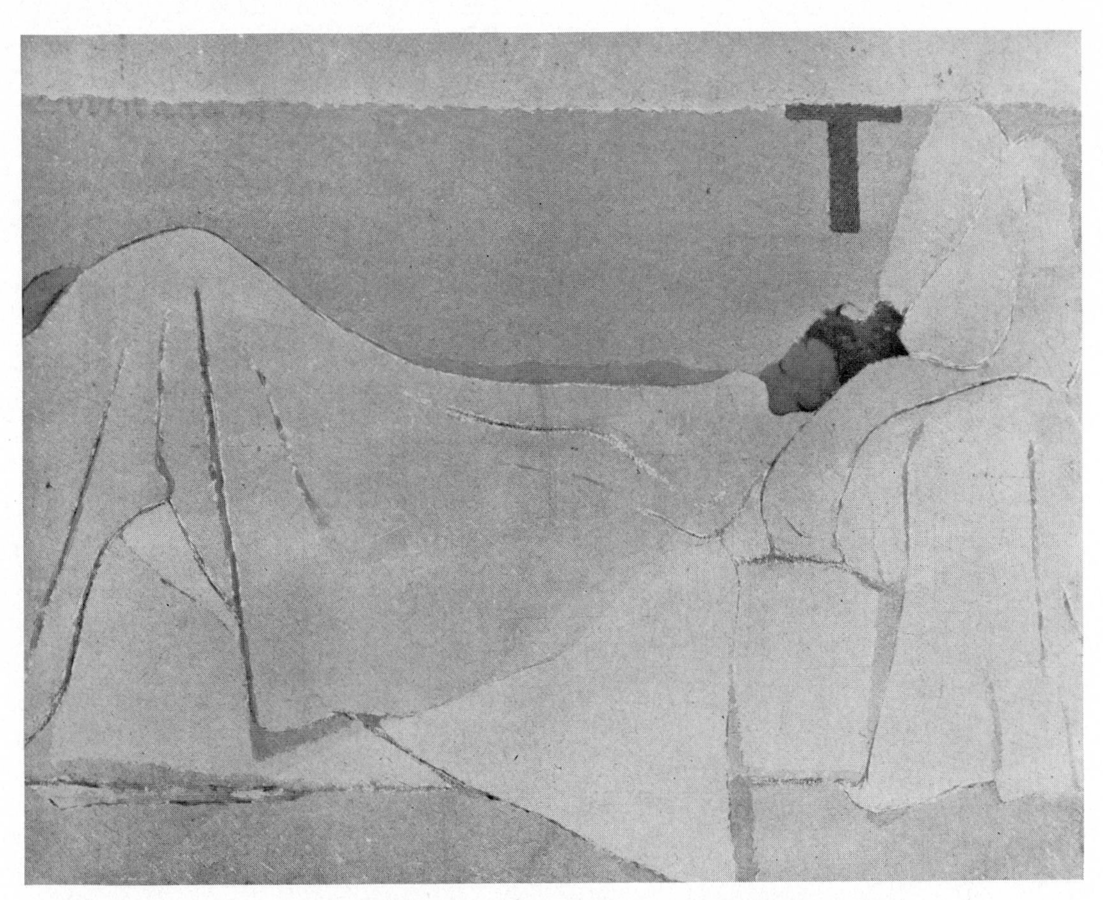

In Bed. 1891. Oil on canvas, 29⅛ x 36¼″. Musée National d'Art Moderne, Paris

The Wood. c. 1892. Oil on board, 6⅝ x 9⅛″. Collection Alex Lewyt, New York

The Dressmakers. 1891. Oil on canvas, 18¾ x 21⅝″. Collection Mr. and Mrs. Ira Haupt, New York

The Flowered Dress. 1891. Oil on canvas, 14 ⅞ x 18″. Private collection, New York

Under the Trees. 1894. Distemper on canvas, 84½ x 38½″. The Cleveland Museum of Art. Gift of Hanna Fund

Promenade. 1894. Distemper on canvas, 84½ x 38½". Robert Lee Blaffer Memorial Collection, Museum of Fine Arts of Houston, Texas

The Family after the Meal. c. 1892. Oil on board, 13¼ x 19¾″. Collection Richard A. Peto, Esq., Isle of Wight, England

The Park. 1894. Distemper on canvas, 83 x 62¾″. Collection Mr. and Mrs. William B. Jaffe, New York

The Dressmaker. 1892. Oil on canvas, 9½ x 13½″. Collection Stephen C. Clark, New York

Two Women by Lamplight. 1892. Oil on canvas, 12½ x 15¾″. Musée de l'Annonciade à Saint-Tropez, France

Theatre Aisle with Toulouse-Lautrec. c. 1892. Oil on canvas, 10½ x 8¼″. Collection Professor and Mrs. Raphael Salem, Cambridge, Mass.

Self Portrait in a Straw Hat. c. 1892. Oil on canvas, 14¼ x 11″. Collection Mr. and Mrs. Ralph F. Colin, New York

Railroad Station. 1892. Oil on canvas, 16 x 13″. Collection Mr. and Mrs. David Rockefeller, New York

Portrait of the Artist's Mother. c. 1897. Oil on board, 14⅛ x 11½″. Collection Mr. and Mrs. William B. Jaffe, New York

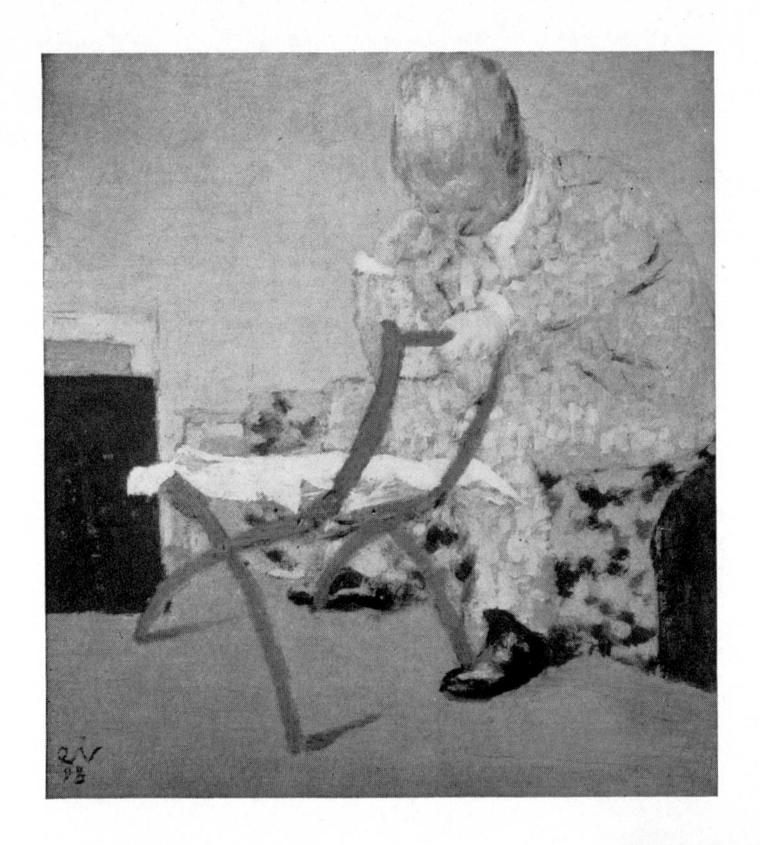

Reading. 1893. Oil on board, 11 x 11″. Collection Philip L. Goodwin, New York

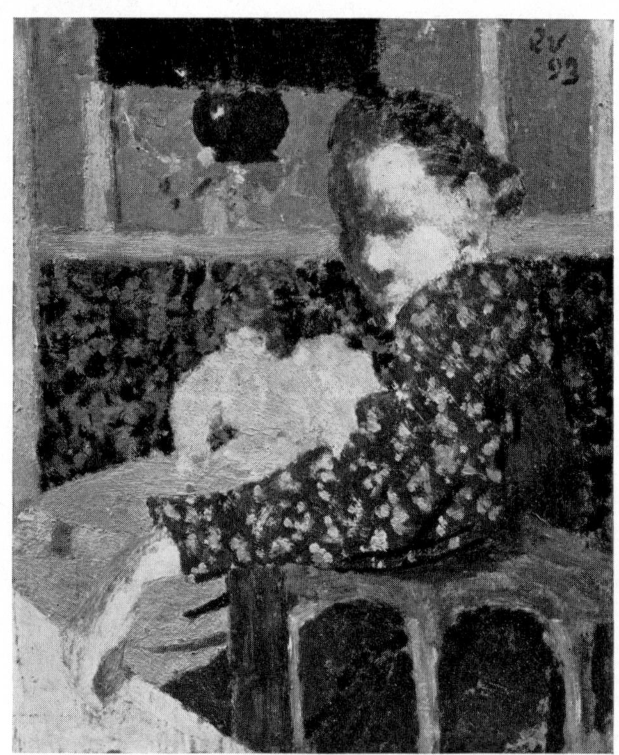

Woman in Blue. 1893. Oil on canvas, 10¼ x 8¾″. Wildenstein & Co., Inc., New York

Vuillard Family at Lunch. 1896. Oil on canvas, 12½ x 18″. Collection Mr. and Mrs. Ralph F. Colin, New York

Conversation. c. 1893. Oil on paper, 19¾ x 24¾″. Art Gallery of Toronto, Canada

Room under the Eaves. 1897. Oil on board, 18 x $25\frac{3}{4}$". Jacques Seligmann & Co., Inc., New York

Breakfast. 1893. Oil on board, 10 x 14″. Collection Mr. and Mrs. Leigh B. Block, Chicago

Woman with a Bowl. c. 1897. Oil on board, 23¼ x 21¼″. Collection André Meyer, New York

Interior at l'Etang la Ville. 1893. Oil on board, 12½ x 14⅜″. Smith College Museum of Art, Northampton, Mass.

Mother and Baby. c. 1899. Oil on board, 20 x 23″. Glasgow Art Gallery, Scotland

Woman Sweeping in a Room. c. 1892-93. Oil on board, 18 x 19″. The Phillips Gallery, Washington, D.C.

Missia and Thadée Natanson. c. 1897. Oil on canvas, 41 x 28″. Collection Mr. and Mrs. Nate B. Spingold, New York

Portrait of the Artist's Grandmother. 1894. Oil on canvas, 25 x 21″. Collection Mr. and Mrs. Gustave Ring, Washington, D. C.

The Bench. 1895. Oil on board, 14¾ x 21½″. Collection Georges Renand, Paris

Mallarmé's House at Valvins. 1895. Oil on board, 7¼ x 15¾″. Collection Jacques Laroche, Paris

Woman Sewing. 1895. Oil on board, 12¾ x 14¾″. Museum of Fine Arts, Boston

Mother and Child. c. 1900. Oil on board, 20⅛ x 19¼″. Collection William Goetz, Los Angeles

Interior with Cipa Godebski and Missia. c. 1895. Oil on board, 24 x 20″. Collection Sir Alexander Korda, London

Mystery. c.1895. Oil on board, 14⅛ x 15⅛″. Carstairs Gallery, New York

The Green Lamp. c. 1895. Oil on board, 14 x 27¼″. Collection Richard A. Peto, Esq., Isle of Wight, England

Family at Table. c. 1897. Oil on board, 19 x 27″. Collection Mr. and Mrs. Fernand Leval, New York

Café Scene. c. 1895. Oil on board, 12 x 11″. Collection Leonard C. Hanna, Jr., Cleveland, Ohio

The Luncheon. 1897. Oil on board, 12⅝ x 21¾″. Paul Rosenberg & Co., New York

The Art Talk. 1898. Distemper on board, 10¾ x 15¾″. Collection Mr. and Mrs. Leon A. Mnuchin, New York

The Ferryman. 1897. Oil on board, 20½ x 29½". Musée National d'Art Moderne, Paris

Woman Seated in a Room. 1899. Oil on canvas, 28 x 27″. Hillman Periodicals, Inc., New York

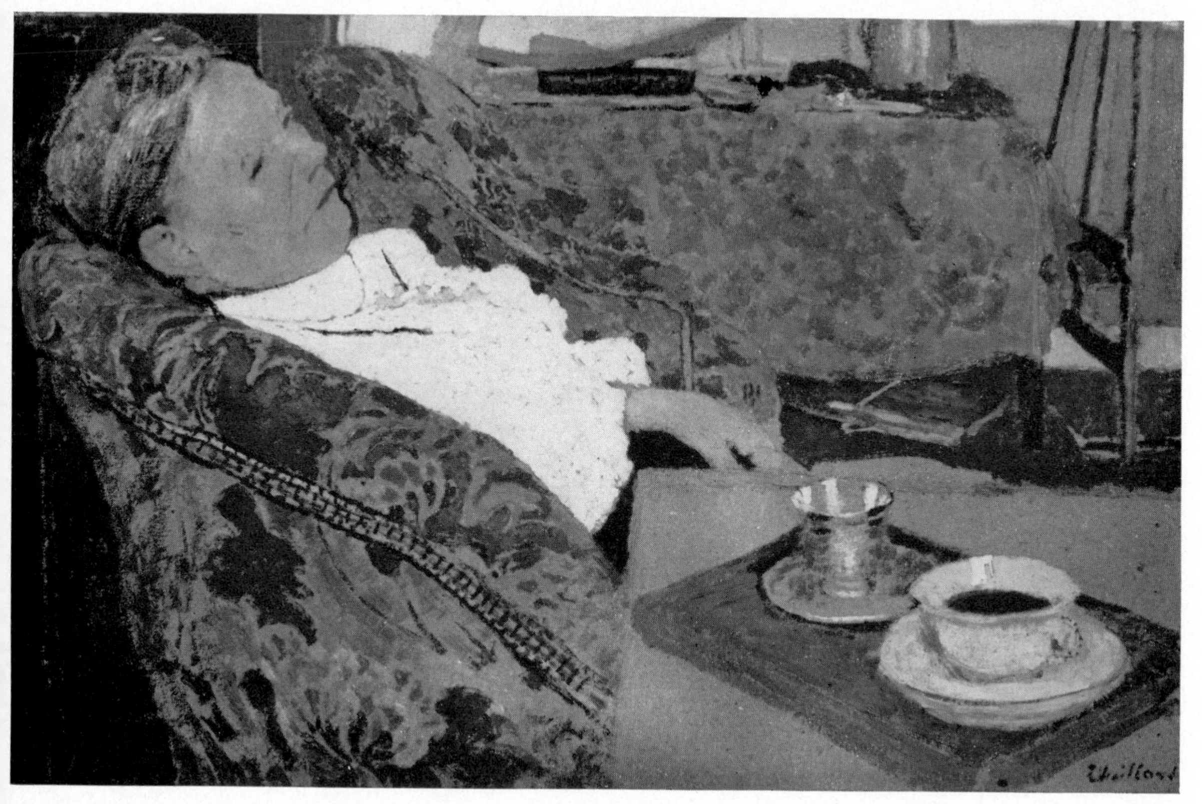

Artist's Mother Resting. c. 1897. Oil on board, 14 x 22″. Estate of Millicent A. Rogers

The Reader (Vaquez decoration). 1896. Distemper on canvas, 82 x 60″. Musée du Petit Palais, Paris. (Not in the exhibition)

The Piano (Vaquez decoration). 1896. Distemper on canvas, 82 x 60″. Musée du Petit Palais, Paris. (Not in the exhibition)

Woman Reading in a Garden. 1898. Distemper on canvas, 84½ x 63⅜″. Collection James Dugdale, Esq., of Crathorne, England

Woman Seated in a Garden. 1898. Distemper on canvas, 84½ x 63⅜″. Collection James Dugdale, Esq., of Crathorne, England

Alfred Natanson and his Wife. 1900. Oil on paper, 21¼ x 26½″. Collection Mr. and Mrs. Nate B. Spingold, New York

The Newspaper. c. 1898. Oil on board, 13½ x 21½″. The Phillips Gallery, Washington, D. C.

Conversation (Cipa and Missia Godebski). 1899. Oil on board, 15½ x 19¾″. Collection Mr. and Mrs. Jacques Gelman, Mexico City

The Natanson Brothers, Missia, and Léon Blum. c. 1898-1900. Oil on board, 17 x 20″. Collection Diane Esmond Wallis, New York

Self Portrait. 1903. Oil on board, 16⅛ x 13⅛". Collection Mr. and Mrs. Donald S. Stralem, New York

Above: *The Meal.* c. 1899. Oil on canvas, 27½ x 28″. Collection Henry P. McIlhenny, Philadelphia

Mother in Profile. c. 1898. Oil on canvas, 13 x 14⅞″. Collection Mr. and Mrs. John Hay Whitney, New York

Child in a Room. c. 1900. Oil on board, 17⅛ x 23¾″. The Art Institute of Chicago

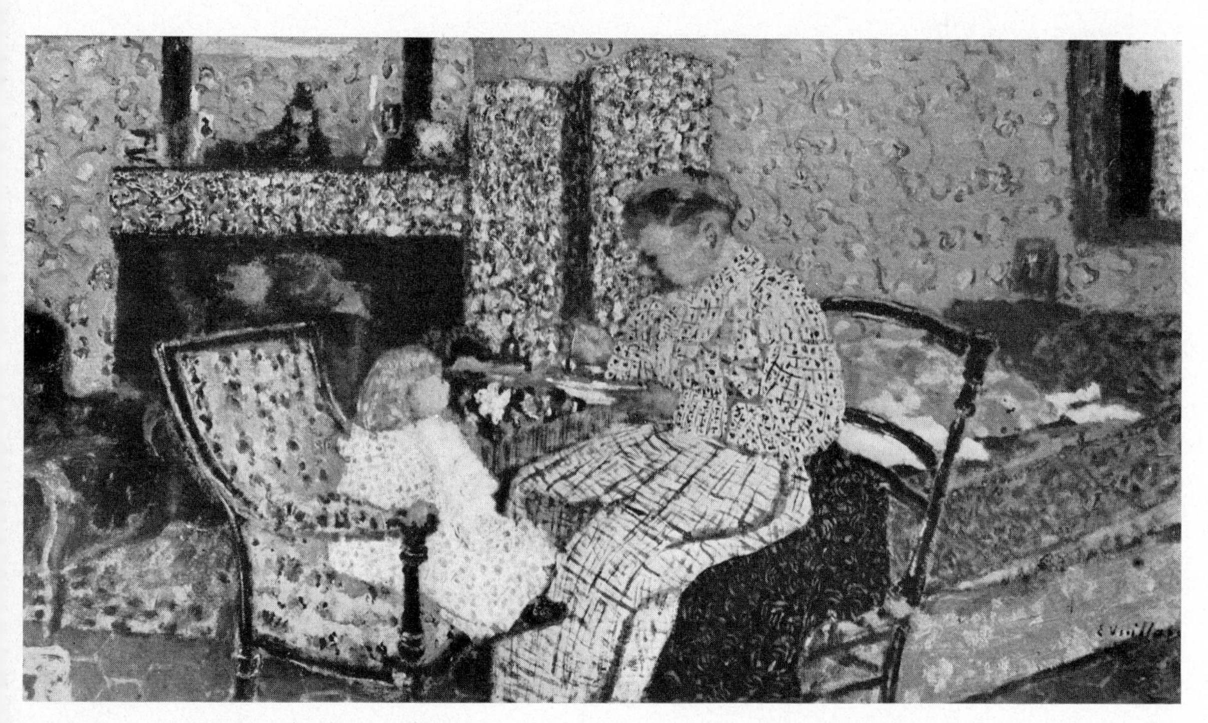

Annette's Lunch. 1901. Oil on board, 13½ x 24″. Musée de l'Annonciade à Saint-Tropez, France

The Painter Ker-Xavier Roussel and his Daughter. c. 1902. Oil on board, 22½ x 20½". Room of Contemporary Art, Albright Art Gallery, Buffalo, N. Y.

Portrait of the Painter Roussel. 1898. Oil on board, 25½ x 17″. Collection Mr. and Mrs. Ralph F. Colin, New York

Near Criquebeuf. 1905. Oil on board, 17¾ x 23¾″. Collection Richard S. Zeisler, New York

View from the Artist's Studio. c. 1906. Oil on canvas, 16¾ x 13½″. Collection Sam Salz, New York

View in Switzerland. 1900. Oil on board, 16 x 32¼″. Private collection, New York

View from the Artist's Studio, rue de la Pompe. c. 1905. Oil on canvas, 28 x 62″. Collection Mr. and Mrs. Harry Lynde Bradley, Milwaukee

The Chaise Longue. c. 1900. Distemper on board, 23¾ x 24⅞″. Collection Mr. and Mrs. Richard Rodgers, New York

Girl with a Doll. 1906. Oil on canvas, 19 x 23¾″. Collection Mr. and Mrs. Leo Glass, New York

Le Square Vintimille. 1908-1917. Distemper on canvas, $63\frac{1}{2}$ x 90″. Collection Mrs. Daniel Wildenstein, New York

The Art Dealers. 1908. Oil on canvas, 28⅞ x 26″. Collection Mr. and Mrs. Richard K. Weil, St. Louis

Interior. 1903. Distemper on board, 31½ x 37½″. Collection Mr. and Mrs. Morris Sprayregen, New York

Scene from Molière's "Le Malade Imaginaire." 1913. Distemper on canvas, 71 x 118″. Decoration for the foyer of the *Comédie des Champs-Elysées,* Paris

Scene from Tristan Bernard's "Le Petit Café." 1913. Distemper on canvas, 71 x 110¼″. Decoration for the foyer of the *Comédie des Champs-Elysées,* Paris

Dr. Gosset Operating. 1912, 1936. Distemper on canvas, 64 x 91″. Private collection, France

Dr. Louis Viau in his Office. 1937. Distemper on board, 36¼ x 33″. Private collection, Corsica

Madame Bénard. c. 1930. Distemper on canvas, 44⅛ x 39⅜″. Musée National d'Art Moderne, Paris

The Window. c. 1914. Distemper on board, 32⅝ x 21¼″. Collection Alex Lewyt, New York

Study for Portrait of Pierre Bonnard. 1925. Distemper on paper, 45 x 56¼″.
Musée du Petit Palais, Paris

Study for Portrait of Maurice Denis. 1925. Distemper on paper, 44 x 54″.
Musée du Petit Palais, Paris

Notes on Vuillard as a Printmaker

One of the many minor factors which loosely gathered the Nabi painters as a group was their common interest in printmaking. Their chief mentor, after Gauguin's escape to Tahiti, became Odilon Redon, an active lithographer since 1879. Toulouse-Lautrec, another friend, had already initiated his famous series of lithographs. The renaissance of lithography in France had even captured a popular audience. Poster designers such as Chéret and Toulouse-Lautrec had wrested the medium from the domination of commercial printers, and their bold inventions could be seen everywhere on the walls and kiosks of Paris. It seems only natural that in the 1890's many of the Nabis, among them Bonnard, Denis, Roussel and Vuillard, should have begun to work on stone. By 1895 they had found in the dealer Ambroise Vollard an editor who was eager to commission and publish their lithographs. Of the Nabis only Vallotton concentrated on the woodcut.

Artists such as Denis and Vallotton were unable to carry into the twentieth century the brilliance of their earlier style as painters or their former production as printmakers. It is interesting that the majority of Vuillard's prints also belong to the decade of the 1890's.

In the winter of 1892-93 Vuillard began the study of lithography in the studio of the master printer Ancourt where both Toulouse-Lautrec and Bonnard were accustomed to work. During the next four years he drew about thirty subjects mostly in black and white but occasionally in two or three colors. Lithographs printed in black such as *Interior* (p. 93) and *Intimacy,* whose very titles might characterize Vuillard's art, are much more successful than any of his first experiments in color. And often, sometimes by scratching into the stone itself, he achieved an airy delicacy never equalled by Bonnard in black and white.

Many of Vuillard's smaller lithographs were published by the magazine the *Revue Blanche* or issued as programs for theatrical productions of *L'Oeuvre* (p. 94). Four of Vuillard's programs are for plays by Ibsen and, among other playwrights, appear Strindberg and Hauptmann. These programs for *L'Oeuvre* were usually so composed that Vuillard had space on the same stone to draw an advertisement for the *Revue Blanche.*

Vuillard received his first commission from Ambroise Vollard in 1896, the color lithograph *The Garden of the Tuileries,* issued in an album of twenty-two prints by as many artists. To a similar publication the following year, Vuillard contributed *Children Playing* (p. 94) and, for Vollard's next collection, printed but unfortunately never published, another color lithograph as well as the cover of the album itself.

In his lithographs for Vollard, Vuillard worked exclusively in color. Tech-

Interior with Screen. c. 1893. Lithograph, 9 7/8 x 12 1/8″. The Museum of Modern Art, New York

nically they are often extremely complex, and Vuillard usually employed five or six different stones for the various colors necessary for each print. He was helped by Auguste Clot, the printer most responsible for the success of Vollard's publications.

In February 1899 Vollard exhibited an album of thirteen color lithographs entitled *Paysages et Intérieurs* (pp. 95, 100). This series, his most important work as a printmaker, can be compared only with Bonnard's album *Quelques Aspects de la Vie de Paris,* which had been Vollard's debut as a publisher in 1895. In Vuillard's album, as in several of his other prints, the vivid realization of the out of doors comes as a surprise in relation to his work as a painter.

It was not Vollard but the German scholar and editor Meier-Graefe who commissioned Vuillard's most ambitious lithograph. In 1901 Meier-Graefe published *Germinal,* an imposing album of large-scale prints and reproductions. One of the stellar contributions was Vuillard's *The Garden outside the Studio,* more than two by one and one-half feet, printed in eight colors. Lithographs by Vuillard were also included in two other German albums of fine prints, *Pan* and *Insel,* as well as in *L'Oeuvre* and *L'Estampe Originale,* published in Paris.

During the 1890's Vuillard had drawn fifty lithographs, half of which were in color. During the twentieth century he drew less than a dozen, all in black and white. The most curious is a study of Cézanne after a self portrait. Six of the later lithographs belong to *Cuisine,* a collection of recipes printed in 1935 to which de Segonzac and de Villeboeuf each contributed six etchings.

Vuillard's first intaglio print was a portrait of the Belgian painter van Rysselberghe etched around 1898. His other etchings consist of two studies of women, done in 1924 and 1930, and, in 1937, four views of the Square Vintimille

La Vie Muette (program for *l'Oeuvre*). 1894. Lithograph, 12¼ x 9½″. The Museum of Modern Art, New York

Children's Game. 1897. Color lithograph, 10¼ x 17⅝″. The Museum of Modern Art, New York

Interior with Pink Wallpaper I and II. 1899. Two color lithographs, 14 x 11″ each. The Museum of Modern Art, New York. Gift of Mrs. John D. Rockefeller, Jr.

opposite his apartment at the foot of Montmartre. Five of Vuillard's seven etchings, gathered posthumously in 1944, were printed as illustrations for Jean Giraudoux's *Le Tombeau de Edouard Vuillard.*

Before the turn of the century many of the best young French painters had been intrigued by the possibilities of the poster as a form of visual communication. Vuillard, however, attempted only one *affiche*—an advertisement of about 1894 for a beverage whose slogan capitalized on the new vogue for cycling as well as the new taste for apéritifs: "Bicyclists take BECANE—an appetizing liqueur, a reconstructing tonic with a meat base."

Unlike Bonnard, Vuillard did not consistently continue to make prints after 1900. Nor was he attracted to book illustration, although in 1898 Vollard had proposed Mallarmé's *Hérodiade.* Mallarmé wrote to Vollard: "I am glad to know that I am being published, mon cher, by a picture dealer. Don't let Vuillard leave Paris without having given you a favorable reply. To encourage him, say that I am pleased with the length of the poem."

Although limited in quantity and restricted in period, a few of Vuillard's single prints are landmarks in the history of modern printmaking. And in color lithography nothing has ever excelled the brilliance and freshness of his album *Paysages et Intérieurs.*

WILLIAM S. LIEBERMAN

Chronology

1868 Born, November 11, Cuiseaux, Saône-et-Loire. Youngest of family of three. Father a retired colonial army officer. Mother, Marie Michaud, daughter of textile designer and manufacturer. Vuillard's uncle Sorel made designs for cashmere shawls.

1877 Family moves to Paris.

1883 Father dies. Mother sets herself up in business as a dressmaker with two helpers. Workroom in apartment on the rue Daunou, later on ground floor of home on the rue du Marché-Saint-Honoré.

1884 Vuillard meets Roussel, a fellow student at the Lycée Condorcet. Maurice Denis was also a fellow student there, as was Lugné-Poë, who was to become a leading theatre director. Mallarmé taught English in this same lycée, leaving in this year to teach at the Lycée Janson.

1886 At Roussel's instigation begins art studies at the Ecole des Beaux-Arts where Gérôme was the principal teacher.

1888 Changes, with Roussel, to the Académie Julian to join forces with Maurice Denis, Bonnard, Ibels, Vallotton, Ranson and Sérusier. Bouguereau was the chief master at this school. Sérusier returns from visiting Gauguin to expound the latter's synthetist theories.

1889 All these young painters band together under the name of Nabis—a name derived from the Hebrew word for prophet. Gauguin's paintings in the *Peintres symbolistes et synthetistes* exhibition at the Café Volpini of great influence on them.

1890 Vuillard, Bonnard, Denis and Lugné-Poë share a studio at 28 rue Pigalle. Vuillard designs a program for Lugné-Poë's *Théâtre Libre.* Denis publishes the first article of his "Théories" in *Art et Critique.*

1891 Begins exhibiting with the other Nabis at Le Barc de Boutteville's. Also exhibits in the offices of the *Revue Blanche* (founded in this year by the Natanson brothers). At these exhibitions he and his friends were "discovered" by the critics Gustave Geffroy, Arsène Alexandre, Roger Marx and Albert Aurier. Aurier's article *Le Symbolisme en Peinture* published in the March issue of *Mercure de France.* About this time Vuillard begins to attend the famous Tuesday evenings at the home of Mallarmé.

1892 First decorative paintings: six panels and screen for Mme Desmarais, now lost. First comes in contact with the art dealer Jos. Hessel, who was associated with the Bernheim brothers. Hessel, through Vuillard's regard for his wife, increasingly influences Vuillard's career. Exhibition of the Nabis at Le Barc de Boutteville's. Albert Aurier's review appears in article, "Les Symbolistes," in the *Revue Encyclopédique,* 1892, pp. 474-86. Aurier calls Vuillard an "intimiste Verlainien."

1893 Vuillard, Roussel, Bonnard and Ranson work together on the scenery for Ibsen's *Rosmersholm* at Lugné-Poë's new *Théâtre de l'Oeuvre.* Previously the Nabis had collaborated in work for Paul Fort's *Théâtre de l'Art* and the *Théâtre des Marionettes.* Unfortunately all these sets, including those for *Rosmersholm,* have been destroyed. Roussel marries Vuillard's sister, Marie.

1894 Commissioned by Alexandre Natanson, one of the editors of the *Revue Blanche,* to decorate his home. For this purpose Vuillard produces a series of nine large panels representing a synthesis of scenes from the public parks of Paris.

1895 Tiffany shows a series of stained glass windows at the Salon, one designed by Vuillard.

1896 Invited with Lautrec and Bonnard to exhibit with *La Libre Esthétique* in Brussels. Paints four large panels, now in the Petit Palais, for his friend Dr. Vaquez, to decorate the latter's drawing room in his house on the Boulevard Haussmann. Moves from the rue du Marché-Saint-Honoré to the rue Truffaut in the Batignolles quarter.

1898 Decorations for the novelist Claude Anet. The two most important panels of this series passed into the hands of Princesse Antoine Bibesco and are now the property of James Dugdale, Esq., of Crathorne.

1899 Vollard publishes Vuillard's series of lithographs, *Paysages et Intérieurs.* The Nabis show for the last time together as a group at Durand-Ruel's.

1903-1914 Exhibits with Bernheim-Jeune, irregularly at the *Salon des Indépendants,* and more consistently at the *Salon d'Automne* (until 1911), of which he was one of the founders. Spends his summers in Brittany and Normandy with the Hessels and their friends.

1904 Moves from the rue Truffaut to the rue de la Tour, near the Trocadero.

1908 Paints a series of decorative panels, representing views of Paris, for Henri Bernstein. Moves from the rue de la Tour to the rue de Calais, near the Place Vintimille. Later moves to a house on the Square Vintimille.

1913 Decorations for the foyer of the *Comédie des Champs Elysées*. Visits London and Holland with Bonnard.

1914 Mobilized into the territorial army to serve as a home guard.

1928 Death of his mother.

1930 Visits Spain with Prince Bibesco.

1936 Forty small pictures included in *Peintres de la Revue Blanche*, an exhibition in connection with the celebration of the fiftieth anniversary of symbolism at the Bibliotèque Nationale.

1937 Decoration for the Palais de Chaillot, entitled *Comedy*.

1938 Elected to the *Institut*. Large retrospective exhibition at the Musée des Arts Décoratifs, the selection supervised by himself. Decoration for the Palace of the League of Nations at Geneva; the subject, *Peace Protecting the Muses*.

1940 In poor health, he is persuaded to leave Paris ahead of the German advance, but dies shortly afterwards at La Baule, June 21.

Bibliography

The following is a selection of references favoring items accessible in local collections. Material now in this library is marked *. With a few exceptions, exhibition catalogs and similar texts noted in the standard periodical indexes have been omitted. Since almost all significant citations on Vuillard are contained in the bibliographies specified, no detailed inventory is required for the purpose of the present catalog.

Bernard Karpel, Librarian of the Museum

*1 ARTES (Antwerp). [Vuillard number]. No. 2, 1946. *November issue; articles by C. Roger-Marx, E. Langui; catalog of exhibition at the Fransch-Belgische Kultureel Akkord.*

2 AURIER, G.-ALBERT. Oeuvres posthumes. Paris, Mercure de France, 1893.

*3 BAZIN, GERMAIN. L'Époque impressioniste. 104 p. Paris, Tisné, 1953. *First edition 1947. Bibliography on impressionism, neo-impressionism and symbolism.*

4 BAZIN, GERMAIN. Lautrec raconté par Vuillard. *L'Amour de l'Art* 12 no.4:141-142 Apr 1931. *English summary.*

4a BENDER. Maurice Denis. *In* Thieme, U. & Becker, F. Allgemeines Lexikon der bildenden Künstler. v.9, p.69-71 Leipzig, Seemann, 1913. *Bibliography.*

*5 BENET, RAFAEL. Simbolismo. 203 p. plus 272 illus. Barcelona, Omega, 1953. *Bibliography.*

*6 BERNE. KUNSTHALLE. Die Maler der Revue Blanche: Toulouse-Lautrec und die Nabis. [34]p. 1951. *Exhibition catalog; bibliography.*

*7 BERNHEIM-JEUNE, J. & G., COLLECTION. L'Art moderne. v.2, p.83-86 Paris, Bernheim-Jeune, 1919. *Early critiques by Mirbeau, Fagus, Natanson, Hepp.*

*8 BRUSSELS. PALAIS DES BEAUX-ARTS. Vuillard (1868-1940); préface de Claude Roger-Marx. 32 p. Bruxelles, La Connaissance, 1946.

*9 CHASSÉ, CHARLES. Le Mouvement symboliste dans l'Art du XIXe Siècle. 215 p. Paris, Floury, 1947.

*10 CHASTEL, ANDRÉ. E. Vuillard. *Art News* 52 no. 7 pt. II: 35-57, 180-185 (passim) Nov 1 1953. *Art News Annual no. 23 (1954). Illustrations p.27-34, 39-42, 51, 54.*

*11 CHASTEL, ANDRÉ. Vuillard, 1868-1940. 123 p. Paris, Floury, 1946. *Chronology, list of exhibitions, bibliography.*

*12 COGNIAT, RAYMOND. Décors de Théâtre. [50]p. plus plates Paris, Chroniques du Jour, 1930. *Lists scenic work by Vuillard.*

*13 COOLUS, ROMAIN. Edouard Vuillard. *L'Art Vivant* no. 221:23-36 May 1938.

*14 COQUIOT, GUSTAVE. Cubistes, Futuristes, Passéistes. p. 200-203 Paris, Ollendorf, 1914. *Another edition 1923.*

15 DENIS, MAURICE. L'époque du symbolisme. *Gazette des Beaux-Arts* 76 no. 854: 165-179 Mar 1934.

*16 DENIS, MAURICE. Théories 1890-1910: Du Symbolisme et de Gauguin vers un nouvel Ordre classique. 4. éd. Paris, Rouart & Watelin, 1920. *First edition, 1912; supplemented by "Nouvelles Théories" (1922).*

*17 DORIVAL, BERNARD. Les Étapes de la Peinture française contemporaine. v.1, p.103-180 Paris, Gallimard, 1943. *Bibliography.*

*18 ESCHOLIER, RAYMOND. La Peinture française, XXe Siècle. p.8-26 Paris, Floury, 1937.

*19 FELS, FLORENT. L'Art Vivant de 1900 à nos Jours. p.136-140 Genève, Cailler, 1950.

*20 FOSCA, FRANÇOIS. Edouard Vuillard. *L'Amour de l'Art* 1:127 1920.

*21 GAUTHIER, E. P. Lithographs of the Revue Blanche, 1893-1895. *Magazine of Art* 45:273-278 Oct 1952.

22 GEFFROY, GUSTAVE. Histoire de l'Impressionisme: La Vie artistique. v.2, p.378-382 Paris, Floury, 1893.

*23 GEORGE, WALDEMAR. Vuillard et l'âge heureux. *L'Art Vivant* no.221: 26-36 May 1938.

23a GIDE, ANDRÉ. Promenade au salon d'automne. *Gazette des Beaux-Arts* no.582:479-481 Dec 1905.

*24 GIRAUDOUX, JEAN. Tombeau de Edouard Vuillard. Orné de 5 Gravures originales à l'eau-forte. Pour les Amis de Vuillard. [26]p. including plates [1944].

*25 GOLDWATER, ROBERT. Symbolist art and theater. *Magazine of Art* 39:366-370 Dec 1946.

*26 GROHMANN, WILL. Edouard Vuillard. *In* Thieme, U. & Becker, F. Allgemeines Lexikon der bildenden Künstler. v.34, p.585-586 Leipzig, Seemann, 1940. *Extensive bibliography.*

*27 HESS, WALTER. Die Farbe in der modernen Malerei. p.74-87 München, Universität München, 1950. *On Denis and Sérusier. Unpublished typescript; bibliography.*

*28 HUMBERT, AGNÈS. Le Groupe de Nabis. *Art-Documents* (Genève) no. 31:8-9, 13 Apr 1953; no.34: 15 July 1953; no.37: 1 Oct 1953.

*29 HUYGHE, RENÉ, ed. Histoire de l'Art contemporain: la Peinture. p. 69-96 illus Paris, Alcan, 1935. *"Les Nabis" by Bazin, Chassé, Dupont, Fegdal, Huyghe, Sterling. Biographical and bibliographical notes. Previously published in L'Amour de l'Art, no.4, Apr 1933.*

*30 JOHNSON, UNA E. Ambroise Vollard, Editeur. p.158-162 New York, Wittenborn, 1944.

30a LAROCHE, HENRY-JEAN. Cuisine, Recueil de 117 Recettes. Paris, Arts et Métiers Graphiques, 1935. *Includes 6 lithographs by Vuillard.*

31 LECLÉRE, TRISTAN. Edouard Vuillard. *Art et Décoration* 37:97-106 illus Oct 1920.

32 LUGNÉ-POË, ALEXANDRE. La Parade. 2 vol. Paris, Nouvelle Revue française, 1930-32.

33 MARGUÉRY, HENRI. Les Lithographies de Vuillard. [32]p. Paris, L'Amateur d'Estampes, 1935. *Previously published in L'Amateur d'Estampes no.5-6 Oct-Dec 1934.*

*34 MEIER-GRAEFE, JULIUS. *Entwicklungsgeschichte der modernen Kunst.* v.1, p.171-175 Stuttgart, Hoffmann, 1904. *Second edition, 1927.*

*35 MELLERIO, ANDRÉ. La Lithographie originale en Couleurs. p.7, 11, 14, 28, 30 Paris, L'Estampe et L'Affiche, 1898.

*36 MELLERIO, ANDRÉ. Le Mouvement idéaliste en Peinture. 72 p. Paris, Floury, 1896.

*37 MELLOT, DENISE, ed. Vuillard dans ses lettres. *Arts* no. 160:8 illus Apr 2 1948.

*38 MERCANTON, JACQUES. Vuillard, et le Goût de Bonheur. 10 p. plus 10 col. plates Paris, Skira, 1949.

*39 NATANSON, THADÉE. Peints à leur Tour. p.364-383 Paris, Michel, 1948.

40 NATANSON, THADÉE. Un groupe de peintres. *La Revue Blanche* v.5 Nov 1893. *Additional references: Apr. 15, 1898; May 1 1900; May 1 1901.*

*41 NATANSON, THADÉE. Sur Edouard Vuillard. *Arts et Métiers Graphiques* no. 65:38-40 Nov 1938.

*42 NATANSON, THADÉE. Sur une exposition des peintres de la Revue Blanche. *Arts et Métiers Graphiques* no. 54:9-18 Aug 15 1936.

*43 PARIS. MUSÉE DES ARTS DÉCORATIFS. Exposition E. Vuillard, mai-juillet. 56 p. illus 1938.

44 PUVIS DE CHAVANNES, HENRI. Un entretien avec Vuillard sur Puvis. *La Renaissance* 9 no.2:87-90 Feb 1926.

*45 RAYNAL, MAURICE. Modern Painting, p. 38-39, 322-323 et passim Geneva & New York, Skira, 1953.

46 REWALD, JOHN. Extraits du journal inédit de Paul Signac. *Gazette des Beaux-Arts* 36:97-128 July-Sept. 1949; 39:265-284 Apr 1952. *English summary.*

*47 ROGER-MARX, CLAUDE. Edouard Vuillard. *Le Portique* no.3:47-55 1946.

48 ROGER-MARX, CLAUDE. Edouard Vuillard, 1867-1940. *Gazette des Beaux-Arts* 29:263-277 June 1946.

49 ROGER-MARX, CLAUDE. Edouard Vuillard à l'Institut. *La Renaissance* 21:67-69 Mar 1938. *English Summary, p.74. Also see Bulletin de l'Institut for Vuillard's "Les envois des pensionnaires de l'Académie de France à Rome en 1938" and "en 1939."*

*50 ROGER-MARX, CLAUDE. Les premières époques de Vuillard. *Art et Industrie* no.2:67-70 Feb 1946.

*51 ROGER-MARX, CLAUDE. L'Oeuvre gravé de Vuillard. [182]p. including plates [Paris &] Monte Carlo, Sauret, 1948.

*52 ROGER-MARX, CLAUDE. Vuillard: his Life and Work. 211 p. New York, La Maison Française and London, P. Elek, 1946. *Bibliography, p. 209-210. Translation of French edition: Paris, Arts et Métiers Graphiques, 1945. Another monograph (76 p.) issued 1948.*

*53 SALOMON, JACQUES. Auprès de Vuillard. 120 p. Paris, La Palme, 1953.

*54 SALOMON, JACQUES. Vuillard: Témoignage de Jacques Salomon. 151 p. Paris, Michel, 1945. *"Notes," p.143-146.*

*55 SAN LAZZARO, G. di. Painting in Paris, 1895-1949. p.26-37 New York, Philosophical Library, 1949. *Italian edition: Roma, Danesi, 1945.*

56 SEGARD, ACHILLE. Peintres d'Aujourd'hui—les Décorateurs. v.2, p.247-303, 320-322 Paris, Ollendorf, 1914.

*57 SÉRUSIER, PAUL. ABC de la Peinture, suivi d'une Étude sur la Vie et l'Oeuvre de Paul Sérusier par Maurice Denis. 123 p. Paris, Floury, 1942. *First edition 1921. Another edition issued 1950, with correspondence collected by Mme Sérusier.*

*58 STRECKER, PAUL. Edouard Vuillard. *Das Kunstwerk* 6 no. 3:19-20 1952. *Followed page 21-23 by "Paul Sérusier und die Schule von Pont Aven" (H. Troendle).*

59 VEBER, PIERRE. Mon ami Vuillard. *Nouvelles Littéraires* no.811:6 Apr 30 1938.

*60 VENTURI, LIONELLO. Impressionists and Symbolists. 244 p. New York, London, Scribner, 1950.

61 VERKADE, Dom WILLIBRORD. Yesterdays of an Artist-Monk. London, Burns, Oates & Washbourne, New York, Kenedy, 1930. *Translated from the German. Best edition: Le Tourment de Dieu: Étapes d'un Moine Peintre (Paris, Rouart & Watelin, 1923).*

*62 VUILLARD, EDOUARD. Cahier de Dessins. Notice de Jacques Salomon; préface de Annette Vaillant. [16]p. plus 50 plates Paris, Quatre Chemins, 1950.

63 VUILLARD, EDOUARD. Paysages et Intérieurs [Douze lithographies en couleurs]. Paris, Vollard, 1899. *Also cover.*

*64 VUILLARD, EDOUARD. Peintures, 1890-1930. Introduction de André Chastel. 7p. plus 16 col. plates Paris, Editions du Chêne, 1948.

*65 WILD, DORIS. Der "intimist" Vuillard als monumental Maler. *Werk* 34 no.12:400-404 Dec 1947. *Also her: Moderne Malerei. p.119-121 Konstanz, Europa, 1950.*

*66 WILDENSTEIN GALLERY, LONDON. Edouard Vuillard. 17 p. 1948. *June exhibit; text by C. Roger-Marx.*

*67 WILENSKI, R. H. Modern French Painters. 424 p. New York, Harcourt, Brace, 1949.

*68 WRIGHT, WILLARD H. Modern Painting. p.164-206 New York & London, Lane, 1915.

Catalog of the Exhibition

Lenders to the Exhibition

Alphonse Bellier, Paris; Mr. and Mrs. Leigh B. Block, Chicago; Mr. and Mrs. Harry Lynde Bradley, Milwaukee; Mr. and Mrs. Sidney F. Brody, Los Angeles; Mr. and Mrs. Albert K. Chapman, Rochester, N. Y.; Stephen C. Clark, New York; Mr. and Mrs. Ralph F. Colin, New York; Mme D. David-Weill, Paris; Gaston T. de Havenon, New York; Peter H. Deitsch, New York; James Dugdale, Esq., of Crathorne, England; Mr. and Mrs. James W. Fosburgh, New York; Mr. and Mrs. Jacques Gelman, Mexico City; Mrs. Charles Gilman, New York; Mr. and Mrs. Leo Glass, New York; William Goetz, Los Angeles; Philip L. Goodwin, New York; Leonard C. Hanna, Jr., Cleveland; Mr. and Mrs. Ira Haupt, New York; Mr. and Mrs. H. Lawrence Herring, New York; Hillman Periodicals, Inc., New York; Mr. and Mrs. William B. Jaffe, New York; Marcel Kapferer, Paris; Sir Alexander Korda, London; Jacques Laroche, Paris; Mr. and Mrs. Fernand Leval, New York; Alex Lewyt, New York; Henry P. McIlhenny, Philadelphia; André Meyer, New York; Mrs. Gerrish Milliken, New York; Mr. and Mrs. Leon A. Mnuchin, New York; Richard A. Peto, Esq., Isle of Wight, England; Georges Renand, Paris; John Rewald, New York; Mr. and Mrs. Gustave Ring, Washington, D. C.; Mr. and Mrs. David Rockefeller, New York; Nelson A. Rockefeller, New York; Mr. and Mrs. Richard Rodgers, New York; Estate of Millicent A. Rogers; Mrs. Nettie Rosenstein, New York; Mr. and Mrs. Walter Ross, New York; Professor and Mrs. Raphael Salem, Cambridge, Mass.; Jacques Salomon, Paris; Mr. and Mrs. Nate B. Spingold, New York; Mr. and Mrs. Morris Sprayregen, New York; Mr. and Mrs. Donald S. Stralem, New York; Diane Esmond Wallis, New York; Mr. and Mrs. Richard K. Weil, St. Louis; Mr. and Mrs. John Hay Whitney, New York; Mrs. Daniel Wildenstein, New York; Richard S. Zeisler, New York.

Albright Art Gallery, Buffalo; The Art Gallery of Toronto; The Art Institute of Chicago; The Cleveland Museum of Art; Glasgow Art Gallery, Scotland; Kunstmuseum, Winterthur, Switzerland; Musée de l'Annonciade à Saint-Tropez, France; Musée National d'Art Moderne, Paris; Musée du Petit Palais, Paris; Museum of Fine Arts, Boston; The Museum of Fine Arts of Houston; The Museum of Modern Art, New York; The Phillips Gallery, Washington, D. C.; Smith College Museum of Art, Northampton, Mass.; Le Théâtre et la Comédie des Champs-Elysées, Paris.

Carstairs Gallery, New York; Fine Arts Associates, New York; Paul Rosenberg & Co., New York; Sam Salz, New York; Jacques Seligmann & Co., New York; Weyhe Gallery, New York; Wildenstein & Co., Inc., New York.

Catalog

The Cleveland Museum of Art: January 26-March 14, 1954

The Museum of Modern Art, New York: April 7-June 6, 1954

In dimensions height precedes width. Items marked with an asterisk are illustrated.

In the designation of media, distemper is used as the English equivalent of the French, détrempe: *colors mixed with glue.*

**Self Portrait in a Mirror.* 1888-90. Signed. Oil on canvas, 17½ x 21⅛″. Lent by Sam Salz, New York. *Color plate p. 11*

**Vuillard and His Friend Varocquez.* 1888-90. Oil on canvas, 36 x 28″. Lent by Alex Lewyt, New York. *Ill. p. 29*

Self Portrait. 1888-90. Oil on canvas, 15¾ x 12¼″. Lent by Jacques Salomon, Paris

Still Life. c. 1889. Signed. Oil on canvas, 8¼ x 12¼″. Lent by Jacques Salomon, Paris

**Bottle with Flowers.* (*La Bouteille avec des fleurs.*) 1889-90. Signed. Oil on canvas, 12½ x 15¾″. Lent by Mr. and Mrs. Donald S. Stralem, New York. *Color plate p. 15*

**Still Life.* 1889-90. Signed. Oil on canvas, 18 x 25½″. Lent by Mr. and Mrs. Nate B. Spingold, New York. *Ill. p. 30*

Still Life with Apple. c. 1890. Signed. Oil on canvas, 13 x 16¼″. Lent by Mr. and Mrs. Ralph F. Colin, New York

**In Bed.* 1891. Signed and dated. Oil on canvas, 29⅛ x 36¼″. Lent by the Musée National d'Art Moderne, Paris. *Ill. p. 31.* New York only

**The Dressmakers.* 1891. Signed. Oil on canvas, 18¾ x 21⅝″. Lent by Mr. and Mrs. Ira Haupt, New York. *Ill. p. 32*

**The Flowered Dress.* 1891. Signed and dated. Oil on canvas, 14⅞ x 18″. Lent anonymously. *Ill. p. 33*

Woman at the Door. 1891. Signed and dated. Oil on board, 11½ x 8″. Lent by Mr. and Mrs. Donald S. Stralem, New York

**Little Girls Walking.* 1891. Signed. Oil on canvas, 32 x 25⅝″. Lent by Mr. and Mrs. Walter Ross, New York. *Color plate p. 17*

**Young Girl Seated.* 1891. Signed. Brush drawing, 7⅞ x 7⅛″. Lent by John Rewald, New York. *Ill. p. 9*

***Figure in a Room.* c. 1891. Signed. Watercolor, 9½ x 5½". Lent by Mr. and Mrs. H. Lawrence Herring, New York. *Ill. p. 18*

**Two Women by Lamplight.* 1892. Signed and dated. Oil on canvas, 12½ x 15¾". Lent by the Musée de l'Annonciade à Saint-Tropez, France. *Ill. p. 38*

The Artist's Mother. 1892. Signed and dated. Wash drawing, 10 x 7½". Lent by John Rewald, New York

**Lilacs.* 1892. Signed. Oil on board, 14 x 11⅛". Lent by Mr. and Mrs. Donald S. Stralem, New York. *Color plate p. 21*

**Railroad Station.* 1892. Signed. Oil on canvas, 16 x 13". Lent by Mr. and Mrs. David Rockefeller, New York. *Ill. p. 40*

Mother in the Kitchen. 1892. Signed. Oil on canvas, 13 x 10". Lent by Sam Salz, New York

Self Portrait. 1892. Oil on board, 14⅛ x 11". Lent by Jacques Salomon, Paris

**The Dressmaker.* 1892. Signed. Oil on canvas, 9½ x 13½". Lent by Stephen C. Clark, New York. *Ill. p. 38*

**Self Portrait.* 1892. Signed. Oil on board, 14 x 11". Lent by Mr. and Mrs. Sidney F. Brody, Los Angeles. *Color frontispiece.* New York only

"Au Divan Japonais." Profile of Yvette Guilbert. 1892. Oil on board, 8 x 8". Lent by Diane Esmond Wallis, New York. New York only

**The Wood.* c. 1892. Signed. Oil on board, 6⅝ x 9⅛". Lent by Alex Lewyt, New York. *Ill. p. 31*

**Self Portrait in a Straw Hat.* c. 1892. Signed. Oil on canvas, 14¼ x 11". Lent by Mr. and Mrs. Ralph F. Colin, New York. *Ill. p. 40*

Breakfast. c. 1892. Signed. Oil on board, 12¾ x 8⅝". Lent by Mr. and Mrs. William B. Jaffe, New York

**Family after the Meal.* c. 1892. Signed. Oil on board, 13¼ x 19¾". Lent by Richard A. Peto, Esq., Isle of Wight, England. *Ill. p. 36*

**Theatre Aisle with Toulouse-Lautrec.* c. 1892. Oil on canvas, 10½ x 8¼". Lent by Professor and Mrs. Raphael Salem, Cambridge, Mass. *Ill. p. 39*

**Woman Sweeping in a Room.* c. 1892-93. Signed. Oil on board, 18 x 19". Lent by The Phillips Gallery, Washington, D. C. *Ill. p. 50*

**Interior at l'Etang la Ville.* 1893. Signed and dated. Oil on board, 12½ x 14⅜". Lent by the Smith College Museum of Art, Northampton, Mass. *Ill. p. 48*

Interior at l'Etang la Ville. 1893. Signed and dated. Oil on canvas, 13 x 16". Lent by Stephen C. Clark, New York

**Woman in Blue.* 1893. Signed and dated. Oil on canvas, 10¼ x 8¾". Lent by Wildenstein & Co., Inc., New York. *Ill. p. 42*

Interior. 1893. Signed and dated. Oil on canvas, 18 x 15". Lent by the Kunstmuseum, Winterthur, Switzerland

**Reading.* 1893. Signed and dated. Oil on board, 11 x 11". Lent by Philip L. Goodwin, New York. *Ill. p. 42*

**Breakfast.* 1893. Signed. Oil on board, 10 x 14". Lent by Mr. and Mrs. Leigh B. Block, Chicago. *Ill. p. 46*

**Symphony in Red.* 1893. Signed. Oil on board, 23 x 25¾". Lent by Mr. and Mrs. Ralph F. Colin, New York. *Color plate p. 28*

**Mother and Sister of the Artist.* c. 1893. Signed. Oil on canvas, 18¼ x 22¼". The Museum of Modern Art, New York. Gift of Mrs. Sadie A. May. *Color plate p. 25*

**The Conversation.* c. 1893. Signed. Oil on paper, 19¾ x 24¾". Lent by The Art Gallery of Toronto, Canada. *Ill. p. 44*

Portrait of Mme Hessel. c. 1893. Signed. Oil on board, 18¾ x 13¾". Lent by Gaston T. de Havenon, New York

The Dressmaker's Shop. c. 1893. Oil on canvas, 18¼ x 45½". Lent by Mr. and Mrs. Walter Ross, New York

**Under the Trees.* 1894. Signed and dated. Distemper on canvas, 84½ x 38½". The Cleveland Museum of Art. Gift of Hanna Fund. *Color plate p. 34*

**Promenade.* 1894. Signed and dated. Distemper on canvas, 84½ x 38½". Lent from the Robert Lee Blaffer Memorial Collection, The Museum of Fine Arts of Houston, Texas. *Color plate p. 35*

**The Park.* 1894. Signed. Distemper on canvas, 83 x 62¾". Lent by Mr. and Mrs. William B. Jaffe, New York. *Color plate p. 37*

**Portrait of the Artist's Grandmother.* 1894. Signed. Oil on canvas, 25 x 21". Lent by Mr. and Mrs. Gustave Ring, Washington, D.C. *Ill. p. 52*

The Little Restaurant. c. 1894. Signed. Oil on board, 11 x 9". Lent by Georges Renand, Paris

**The Bench.* 1895. Signed and dated. Oil on board, 14¾ x 21½". Lent by Georges Renand, Paris. *Ill. p. 53*

**Woman Sewing.* 1895. Signed and dated. Oil on board, 12¾ x 14¾". Lent by the Museum of Fine Arts, Boston, Mass. *Ill. p. 54*

**Mallarmé's House at Valvins.* 1895. Signed and dated. Oil on board, 7¼ x 15¾". Lent by Jacques Laroche, Paris. *Ill. p. 53*

**Café Scene.* c. 1895. Signed. Oil on board, 12 x 11". Lent by Leonard C. Hanna, Jr., Cleveland. *Ill. p. 59*

**The Green Lamp.* c. 1895. Signed. Oil on board, 14 x 27¼". Lent by Richard A. Peto, Esq., Isle of Wight, England. *Ill. p. 57*

**Interior with Cipa Godebski and Missia*. c. 1895. Signed. Oil on board, 24 x 20″. Lent by Sir Alexander Korda, London. *Ill. p. 56*

**Mystery*. c. 1895. Signed. Oil on board, 14⅛ x 15⅛″. Lent by the Carstairs Gallery, New York. *Ill. p. 57*

Black Cat in Courtyard. c. 1895. Signed. Oil on board, 7⅜ x 6¾″. Lent by Mrs. Gerrish Milliken, New York

**Vuillard Family at Lunch*. 1896. Signed. Oil on canvas, 12½ x 18″. Lent by Mr. and Mrs. Ralph F. Colin, New York. *Color plate p. 43*

**The Ferryman*. 1897. Signed and dated. Oil on board, 20½ x 29½″. Lent by the Musée National d'Art Moderne, Paris. *Ill. p. 61*

**Room under the Eaves*. 1897. Signed and dated. Oil on board, 18 x 25¾″. Lent by Jacques Seligmann & Co., Inc., New York. *Color plate p. 45*

**The Luncheon*. 1897. Signed and dated. Oil on board, 12⅝ x 21¾″. Lent by Paul Rosenberg & Co., New York. *Ill. p. 60*

**Missia and Thadée Natanson*. c. 1897. Signed. Oil on canvas, 41 x 28″. Lent by Mr. and Mrs. Nate B. Spingold, New York. *Color plate p. 51*

**The Artist's Mother Resting*. c. 1897. Signed. Oil on board, 14 x 22″. Lent by the Estate of Millicent A. Rogers. *Ill. p. 63*

**Family at Table*. c. 1897. Signed. Oil on board, 19 x 27″. Lent by Mr. and Mrs. Fernand Leval, New York. *Color plate p. 58*

**Portrait of the Artist's Mother*. c. 1897. Signed. Oil on board, 14⅛ x 11½″. Lent by Mr. and Mrs. William B. Jaffe, New York. *Color plate p. 41*

**Woman with a Bowl*. c. 1897. Oil on board, 23¼ x 21¼″. Lent by André Meyer, New York. *Color plate p. 47*. New York only

**Portrait of the Painter Roussel*. 1898. Signed and dated. Oil on board, 25½ x 17″. Lent by Mr. and Mrs. Ralph F. Colin, New York. *Ill. p. 77*

**Woman Reading in a Garden*. 1898. Signed and dated. Distemper on canvas, 84½ x 63⅜″. Lent by James Dugdale, Esq., of Crathorne, England. *Ill. p. 66*

**Woman Seated in a Garden*. 1898. Signed and dated. Distemper on canvas, 84½ x 63⅜″. Lent by James Dugdale, Esq., of Crathorne, England. *Ill. p. 67*

**The Art Talk*. 1898. Signed. Distemper on board, 10¾ x 15¾″. Lent by Mr. and Mrs. Leon A. Mnuchin, New York. *Ill. p. 60*

Missia Natanson Sewing. 1898. Signed. Oil on board, 18 x 19″. Lent by Wildenstein & Co., Inc., New York

An Evening of Music. 1898. Signed. Oil on board, 18 x 22″. Lent by Mr. and Mrs. Donald S. Stralem, New York

**Mother in Profile*. c. 1898. Signed. Oil on canvas, 13 x 14⅞″. Lent by Mr. and Mrs. John Hay Whitney, New York. *Ill. p. 73*

**The Newspaper*. c. 1898. Signed. Oil on board, 13½ x 21½″. Lent by The Phillips Gallery, Washington, D.C. *Ill. p. 69*

**The Natanson Brothers, Missia, and Léon Blum*. c. 1898-1900. Oil on board, 17 x 20″. Lent by Diane Esmond Wallis, New York. *Ill. p. 71*. New York only

The Writer. 1899. Signed. Oil on canvas, 18½ x 22½″. Lent by Mr. and Mrs. Richard K. Weil, St. Louis

**Conversation (Cipa and Missia Godebski)*. 1899. Signed. Oil on board, 15½ x 19¾″. Lent by Mr. and Mrs. Jacques Gelman, Mexico City. *Ill. p. 70*

**Woman Seated in a Room*. 1899. Signed. Oil on canvas, 28 x 27″. Lent by Hillman Periodicals, Inc., New York. *Color plate p. 62*

**The Meal*. c. 1899. Signed. Oil on canvas, 27½ x 28″. Lent by Henry P. McIlhenny, Philadelphia. *Ill. p. 73*. New York only

**Mother and Baby*. c. 1899. Signed. Oil on board, 20 x 23″. Lent by the Glasgow Art Gallery, Scotland. *Color plate p. 49*

**Alfred Natanson and his Wife*. 1900. Signed. Oil on paper, 21¼ x 26½″. Lent by Mr. and Mrs. Nate B. Spingold, New York. *Color plate p. 68*

Woman Sewing, Interior. 1900. Signed. Oil on canvas, 18 x 25½″. Lent by William Goetz, Los Angeles

**View in Switzerland*. 1900. Signed. Oil on board, 16 x 32¼″. Lent anonymously. *Color plate p. 80*

**The Chaise Longue*. c. 1900. Signed. Distemper on board, 23¾ x 24⅞″. Lent by Mr. and Mrs. Richard Rodgers, New York. *Color plate p. 82*

**Mother and Child*. c. 1900. Signed. Oil on board, 20⅛ x 19¼″. Lent by William Goetz, Los Angeles. *Color plate p. 55*

The Arbor. c. 1900. Signed. Distemper on canvas, 23½ x 18½″. Lent by Jacques Laroche, Paris

Mme Vuillard with a Carafe. c. 1900. Signed. Oil on board, 16¾ x 15¾″. Lent by Jacques Laroche, Paris

**Child in a Room*. c. 1900. Oil on board, 17⅛ x 23¾″. Lent by The Art Institute of Chicago. *Ill. p. 74*

**Annette's Lunch*. 1901. Signed. Oil on board, 13½ x 24″. Lent by the Musée de l'Annonciade à Saint-Tropez, France. *Ill. p. 75*

**The Painter Ker-Xavier Roussel and his Daughter*. c. 1902. Signed. Oil on board, 22½ x 20½″. Lent from the Room of Contemporary Art, Albright Art Gallery, Buffalo. *Ill. p. 76*

Woman Reading. 1903. Signed and dated. Oil on canvas, 23½ x 26″. Lent by Mrs. Nettie Rosenstein, New York

**Self Portrait*. 1903. Signed. Oil on board, 16⅛ x 13⅛″. Lent by Mr. and Mrs. Donald S. Stralem, New York. *Color plate p. 72*

**Interior*. 1903. Signed. Distemper on board, 31½ x 37½″. Lent by Mr. and Mrs. Morris Sprayregen, New York. *Color plate p. 86*

Missia at the Piano. 1904. Signed and dated. Oil on board, 20⅞ x 24″. Lent by Paul Rosenberg & Co., New York

Vase of Flowers. 1904. Signed and dated. Oil on board, 23⅝ x 22⅞″. Lent by the Musée National d'Art Moderne, Paris

At the Seashore. c. 1904. Signed. Oil on board, 8½ x 8½″. Lent by Sam Salz, New York

**Near Criquebeuf*. 1905. Signed. Oil on board, 17¾ x 23¾″. Lent by Richard S. Zeisler, New York. *Ill. p. 78*

Le Café Wepler. c. 1905. Signed. Oil on canvas, 24½ x 40⅝″. The Cleveland Museum of Art. Gift of Hanna Fund

Mme Hessel Resting. c. 1905. Signed. Oil on canvas, 17 x 25½″. Lent by Mr. and Mrs. Albert K. Chapman, Rochester, New York

**View from the Artist's Studio, rue de la Pompe*. c. 1905. Oil on canvas, 28 x 62″. Lent by Mr. and Mrs. Harry Lynde Bradley, Milwaukee. *Ill. p. 81*

**Girl with a Doll*. 1906. Signed and dated. Oil on canvas, 19 x 23¾″. Lent by Mr. and Mrs. Leo Glass, New York. *Ill. p. 83*

**View from the Artist's Studio*. c. 1906. Signed. Oil on canvas, 16¾ x 13½″. Lent by Sam Salz, New York. *Ill. p. 79*

Anemones. 1907. Signed and dated. Distemper on board, 21½ x 21″. Lent by Mr. and Mrs. Donald S. Stralem, New York

The Luncheon. 1908. Oil on board, 8½ x 16½″. Lent by Mr. and Mrs. James W. Fosburgh, New York

**The Art Dealers*. 1908. Signed. Oil on canvas, 28⅞ x 26″. Lent by Mr. and Mrs. Richard K. Weil, St. Louis, through the courtesy of the City Art Museum of St. Louis. *Ill. p. 85*

**Le Square Vintimille*. 1908-1917. Signed. Distemper on canvas, 63½ x 90″. Lent by Mrs. Daniel Wildenstein, New York. *Ill. p. 84*. New York only

Interior. c. 1910. Signed. Distemper on board, 45 x 22½″. Lent by the Fine Arts Associates, New York

Annette at Villerville. c. 1910. Distemper on paper, 68½ x 48¾″. Lent by Jacques Salomon, Paris

Child at Lunch. 1911. Signed. Oil on canvas. Lent anonymously

**Dr. Gosset Operating*. 1912, 1936. Signed. Distemper on canvas, 64 x 91″. Lent anonymously. *Ill. p. 88*

**Scene from Tristan Bernard's "Le Petit Café."* 1913. Signed and dated. Distemper on canvas, 71 x 110½″. Lent by Le Théâtre et la Comédie des Champs-Elysées, Paris. *Ill. p. 87*. New York only

**Scene from Molière's "Le Malade Imaginaire."* 1913. Signed and dated. Distemper on canvas, 71 x 118″. Lent by Le Théâtre et la Comédie des Champs-Elysées, Paris. *Ill. p. 87*. New York only

Dr. Georges Viau in his Office. 1914. Signed and dated. Distemper on board, 43¼ x 55⅛″. Lent anonymously

**The Window*. c. 1914. Signed. Distemper on board, 32⅝ x 21¼″. Lent by Alex Lewyt, New York. *Color plate p. 90*

Figures in an Interior. c. 1915. Signed. Distemper on board, 35½ x 31″. Lent by Mrs. Charles Gilman, New York

The Artist's Mother. c. 1917. Signed. Distemper on board, 25 x 23″. Lent by the Estate of Millicent A. Rogers

Dr. Vaquez Operating. c. 1917. Signed. Pastel on paper, 25½ x 20″. Lent by Georges Renand, Paris

Lunch (Mme Vuillard). c. 1917? Signed. Oil on board, 23 x 28¼″. Lent by Alphonse Bellier, Paris

Mme Kapferer. 1919. Signed and dated. Distemper on canvas, 50¾ x 37⅜″. Lent by Marcel Kapferer, Paris

Three drawings for *Dr. Vaquez at the Hospital*. c. 1921. Signed. Pencil on paper, No. 1. 7⅞ x 5″; No. 2. 7⅞ x 4⅞″; No. 3. 7⅞ x 4⅞″. Lent by Georges Renand, Paris

Mme Tristan Bernard in her Drawing Room. 1925. Signed and dated. Oil on canvas, 11½ x 14″. Lent by Alex Lewyt, New York

**Study for Portrait of Maurice Denis*. 1925. Signed. Distemper on paper, 44 x 54″. Lent by the Musée du Petit Palais, Paris. *Ill. p. 91*

**Study for Portrait of Pierre Bonnard*. 1925. Signed. Distemper on paper, 45 x 56¼″. Lent by the Musée du Petit Palais, Paris. *Ill. p. 91*

The Artist's Mother Smiling. c. 1925. Signed. Drawing, 23¾ x 29⅛″. Lent by Jacques Salomon, Paris

In the Studio. c. 1925. Signed. Pastel, 21⅝ x 19¾″. Lent by Mme D. David-Weill, Paris

The Housewife (Mme Vuillard). c. 1925. Signed. Oil on board, 16¼ x 11¼″. Lent by Jacques Laroche, Paris

Siesta. 1928? Signed and dated. Pencil and watercolor, 6¾ x 4⅜″. The Museum of Modern Art, New York. Gift of Sam Salz

Still Life. c. 1928. Signed. Pastel, 20 x 20½″. Lent by Mme D. David-Weill, Paris

**Madame Bénard*. c. 1930. Signed. Distemper on canvas, 44⅛ x 39⅜″. Lent by the Musée National d'Art Moderne, Paris. *Ill. p. 89*

Study for Portrait of the Comtesse de Noailles. c. 1932. Signed. Charcoal on canvas, 43¼ x 50¼″. Lent by the Musée National d'Art Moderne, Paris

Portrait of the Comtesse de Noailles. c. 1932. Signed. Oil on canvas, 43½ x 50½″. Lent by Sam Salz, New York

**Dr. Louis Viau in his Office*. 1937. Signed. Distemper on board, 36¼ x 33″. Lent anonymously. *Ill. p. 89*

Portrait of Sam Salz. 1937. Gouache and pastel, 20 x 13½″. Lent by Sam Salz, New York

Vase of Flowers. Pencil, 6⅝ x 4″. The Museum of Modern Art, New York. Gift of Sam Salz

Prints

The definitive catalog of Vuillard's prints referred to as RM is *L'Oeuvre gravé de Vuillard* by Claude Roger-Marx, see bibl. 51.

Siesta (The Convalescence). 1893. Color lithograph, 11½ x 9″. (RM 2). The Museum of Modern Art, New York. Gift of Mrs. John D. Rockefeller, Jr.

**Interior with Screen*. c. 1893. Lithograph printed in black, 9⅞ x 12⅛″. (RM 8). The Museum of Modern Art, New York. *Ill. p. 93*

"Rosmersholm" (program for *L'Oeuvre*). 1893. Lithograph printed in black, 8¼ x 12¼″. (RM 16). The Museum of Modern Art, New York

*"La Vie Muette" (program for *L'Oeuvre*). 1894. Lithograph printed in black, 12¼ x 9½″. (RM 20). The Museum of Modern Art, New York. *Ill. p. 94*

"Lisez la *Revue Blanche*" and "Au dessus des forces humaines" (program for *L'Oeuvre*). 1894. Two lithographs printed in black from one stone, 12 x 18¾″. (RM 18). The Museum of Modern Art, New York

Intimacy. c. 1894. Lithograph printed in black, 10⅜ x 7⅞″. (RM 10). The Museum of Modern Art, New York

The Dressmaker. 1894. Color lithograph, 9¾ x 6⅜″. (RM 13). The Museum of Modern Art, New York

The Tuileries. 1895. Lithograph printed in green, 9½ x 10¾″. (RM 27). Lent by Nelson A. Rockefeller, New York

The Garden of the Tuileries. 1896. Color lithograph, 11⅛ x 17″. (RM 28). Lent by the Weyhe Gallery, New York

Mother and Child. 1896. Color lithograph, 7½ x 9″. (RM 30). The Museum of Modern Art, New York

**Children's Game*. 1897. Color lithograph, 10¼ x 17⅝″. (RM 29). The Museum of Modern Art, New York. *Ill. p. 94*

Cover for *L'Album des Peintres-Graveurs*. 1898. Color lithograph, 23½ x 18″. (RM 47). The Museum of Modern Art, New York

From *Paysages et Intérieurs*. An album of 13 color lithographs. The Museum of Modern Art, New York. Gift of Mrs. John D. Rockefeller, Jr.

- Cover. 1899. Color lithograph, 20 9/16 x 15⅞″. (RM 31)
- *The Game of Checkers*. 1899. Color lithograph, 14⅜ x 11″. (RM 32)
- *The Avenue*. 1899. Color lithograph, 12⅜ x 16 5/16″. (RM 33)
- *Across the Fields*. 1899. Color lithograph, 10⅛ x 14⅜″. (RM 34)
- **Interior with Pink Wallpaper I*. 1899. Color lithograph, 14 x 11″. (RM 36). *Ill. p. 95*
- **Interior with Pink Wallpaper II*. 1899. Color lithograph, 14 x 11″. (RM 37). *Ill. p. 95*
- *The Hearth*. 1899. Color lithograph, 14½ x 10⅞″. (RM 39)
- *Two Girls on the Pont de L'Europe*. 1899. Color lithograph, 12⅛ x 15″. (RM 40)
- *Café Terrace at Night*. 1899. Color lithograph, 14⅝ x 11 1/16″. (RM 41)
- *The Cook*. 1899. Color lithograph, 14⅛ x 10⅞″. (RM 42)
- *The Two Sisters-in-Law*. 1899. Color lithograph, 14½ x 11½″. (RM 43)

The Birth of Annette. c. 1899. Color lithograph, 13⅜ x 15¾″. (RM 44). Lent by Peter H. Deitsch, New York

A Balcony at the Gymnasium. 1900. Color lithograph, 10 x 7⅞″. (RM 48). The Museum of Modern Art, New York

The Garden outside the Studio. 1901. Color lithograph, 24¾ x 18⅞″. (RM 45). Lent by Nelson A. Rockefeller, New York

Portrait of Cézanne. 1914. Lithograph printed in black, 9 x 9½″. (RM 51). The Museum of Modern Art, New York

Tombeau de Edouard Vuillard, a book by Jean Giraudoux (see bibl. 24). Contains 5 etchings, 1898 to 1937, printed posthumously. (RM 61, 62, 64, 65, 66). The Museum of Modern Art, New York